A Room Full of Tears
I Never Cried

A Room Full of Tears
I Never Cried

By
Ronald Weidner

XULON PRESS

Xulon Press
2301 Lucien Way #415
Maitland, FL 32751
407.339.4217
www.xulonpress.com

© 2020 by Ronald Weidner

All rights reserved solely by the author. The author guarantees all contents are original and do not infringe upon the legal rights of any other person or work. No part of this book may be reproduced in any form without the permission of the author. The views expressed in this book are not necessarily those of the publisher.

Unless otherwise indicated, Scripture quotations taken from the New King James Version (NKJV). Copyright © 1982 by Thomas Nelson, Inc. Used by permission. All rights reserved.

Printed in the United States of America.

Paperback ISBN-13: 978-1-6322-1304-4
eBook ISBN-13: 978-1-6322-1305-1

Table of Contents

1. Don't Go, A Storm is Coming..................1
2. Tribute To My Father..................5
3. Memories You Can't Out Run..................9
4. A Sign of His Presence..................13
5. Choices in Tragedy..................16
   a. Well of Bitterness..................17
   b. Well of Living Water..................18
6. Conceived in Love/Born in Tragedy..................21
7. From Death Pains to Birth Pains..................25
8. Pool Halls Plus Swearing Equals Orange Pop..................28
9. Broken Hearts Merge..................32
10. Theological Ideologies Clash..................36
11. A Stranger Among Us..................39
12. A Kindergarten Drop Out..................44
13. Life on the Farm..................51
14. Learning the Meaning of Hard Work..................56
15. Pressure to Perform..................64
16. Troubled Teens..................67
    a. Life without boundaries..................67
    b. A philosophy to live by..................71
17. A Blond Joke..................79
18. I Saw the "Light"..................85
19. Graduated From High School, Now What?..................89
20. A Whole New World..................93

21. Lessons Learned in College 98
22. A College Degree in One Hand/Marriage License in
    the Other 100
23. "I Wanna Go Home" 104
24. Not Qualified 106
25. A Mighty Move For the House of the Lord 108
26. Ron and the Peter Principle 113
27. Resigned Only To Be Fired 116
28. Back To My Roots... a Disaster in the Making 119
29. Income From Nowhere 124
30. The Lord Sends A Ladder 127
31. From Bad to Worse 131
32. A Tribute To My Mother 133
33. Getting the Cobwebs Out 138
34. Candle Lighters 141
35. A Room Full of Tears I Never Cried 145
36. When the Body Cries Out 148
37. Health Issues 150
    a. Appendectomy and a confession 150
    b. A body used and abused 151
    c. Dying inside 153
    d. A walking dead man 155
    e. Sleep driving 157
    f. Orders to unplug all the machines 160
    g. 3 Tries to get it right 161
38. What I Have Learned From A Higher View 164
39. Joys in My Life 170
    a. Acting 170
    b. Grandchildren 173
    c. Fishing 181
    d. The God Pocket 185
40. About the Author 188

Preface

Over the years many individuals have encouraged me to write my life story down in book form. For years, I was able to brush that thought off by telling myself no one would really care about my life. I have always thought every person has their own story to tell, but friends kept encouraging me, telling me that my story is unique and needs to be told.

I remember the moment not so long ago when the Spirit of God clearly spoke to me and said, "I haven't allowed you to experience everything in life for you to waste it and not share with others." It is with that leading that I now want to share with you my spiritual journey which includes my many spiritual flaws.

My desire is to share with you the many "speed bumps" I faced, both before Christ and those after finding my faith in Christ. Some people might call these bumps "road blocks". No matter what we call it, I believe that God has a way of trying to get our attention and point out when we are on the wrong road. There is no question that I was on the wrong road many times, but God never gave up on me as he continued to call me back to Himself.

The hardest part of writing my story is going back and remembering the different events and the emotions that I experienced. Much of the past has been locked, or so I thought, in my sub-conscious mind, but as I began to write, the Spirit gave insight to a lot of emotions that were long ago blocked. In a way the sharing of this emotional journey has been a therapeutic experience.

Without the support of my "Monday morning coffee partners" who encouraged me from the beginning, my family who has stuck with me through every trial, every surgery, and my many shortcomings, and especially my grandkids who have no idea how much I have learned from them, none of this would have been possible. I now give praise, honor and glory to my Lord and Savior who loved me when I was so unlovely. He showed me what it means to serve others and died for me so that my name is now in the "Lamb's Book of Life." Special thanks to Kristi Wallman and Avery Shumaker for helping with sentence structure, punctuation, grammar, editing, and technical help. I could not have done this alone.

1

Don't Go, A Storm is Coming

Excitement and the smell of harvest filled the air. It was time to gather the shocks of grain and begin thrashing. With several farmers getting together to help one another, it was time to work and visit. The women would be busy preparing food and then feeding the large thrashing crew. Farmers everywhere were getting chores done early so they could get to the farm site where they were thrashing that day. One farmer in particular got up earlier than usual, because the crew was coming to his farm that day to thrash. There were cows to be milked and he wanted that done before anyone arrived.

As his wife looked out the window, she noticed a small rain cloud approaching quite fast from the west and getting closer. She told her husband that he should wait until it passed because it might rain and harvesting for the day would be delayed or even canceled. Her husband was determined not to cause a delay in harvesting by not having his chores done. In spite of her last words to him, he decided to go undeterred by his wife's concern over a little cloud. He left the house hearing her plea. "Don't go, a storm is coming!"

After some time, the eerie silence of the early morning was interrupted by a flash of light and an immediate vibration. The rumbling rattled windows for miles around. In that fraction of a second, life for that farm family would change forever.

Neighbors from across the road saw the flash of light, and they immediately heard the rumble, and they came running across the road to see what had just happened. As they approached, they noticed three cows on the ground, kicking and trying to get up. The neighbors stood watching for a while until the cows finally were able to get up and walk off into the pasture. By this time, there were other men arriving in the yard to check things out. Several men soon found their neighbor's lifeless body lying on the ground. With heavy hearts, the men carried their neighbor up to the house and laid him in the porch. As they quickly laid his lifeless body down, they witnessed a black hole on one side of his temple and blood was draining from his eyes.

I can only imagine his wife, who was seven months with child, insisted on seeing him. I do not know for sure if she saw him, but knowing the extreme shock and prolonged emotional trauma she endured, I believe she must have seen his face. Inside the house were the couple's two sons and one daughter. The shock, the horror, and the reality of what had just happened is more than can be put into words. Tragedy had struck this farm family that morning and all the hopes, dreams and plans for each of their lives were forever shattered. The life of each family member from that day on would forever be changed in ways no one could imagine. Each family member, although not all remembering that day, would bear the scars of the outcome and would have to deal with it in their own way.

The wife and the three kids were taken to the neighbor's house as the wife dealt with her grief that tore at the core of her soul. There are no words that I could write to describe what this wife must of felt as her world seem to be falling apart. I know that all I have described about that day is true, because the farmer lying on the porch floor that day was my father, Abraham Weidner, aged 29 years 6 months and 3 days. The two boys and the one girl inside where my brothers and my sister, and that farmer's unborn child was me.

Where was God?

Throughout eternity men and women have asked why bad things happen, and they question where God was in all of this. In looking back on that day, I do not ask this question in a negative way, but rather I look at ways that God uses tragedy to help each of us. I find it very helpful to look at the reasons and ways God might use suffering described in later chapter. Isaiah 55:8 reminds us, "For my thoughts are not your thoughts, neither are your ways my ways," declares the LORD.

Abraham Weidner

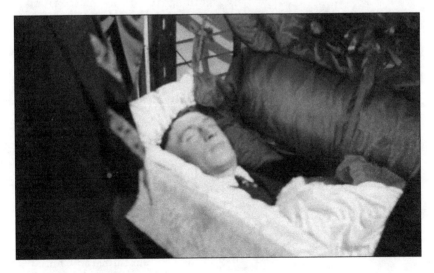

Lightning Kills Huron Farmer

Abraham Wiedner, 29, was killed by lightning at 7:30 a. m. today on his farm about 15 miles northeast of Huron.

Wiedner was driving the cows to pasture when the lightning struck him about 15 feet from a steel water tank.

He is survived by his wife and three children, a daughter, Dianna Ray, 3; and two sons, Quinton Lee, 6, and Larry Dean, 4.

No arrangements for the funeral have been made.

Hold Funeral Services For Wiedner Friday

Funeral services for Abraham Wiedner, who was killed by lightning on his farm about 15 miles northeast of Huron early Tuesday morning, will be held at 2 p. m. Friday in the German Lutheran Church of Yale with the Rev. L. K. Meyer officiating.

Burial will be in the Lutheran Cemetery near Yale.

He is survived by his wife and three children, a daughter, Dianna Ray, 3, and two sons, Quinton Lee, 6, and Larry Dean, 4.

2

Tribute To My Father

I know that I could never do justice to describe the man I never knew. In my heart, I want very much to believe what others have told me about him. Dads are supposed to be heroes to their sons. Visiting with those who were alive at the time of the accident has given me enough information to conclude my dad would have been a real hero in my life. My dad, Abraham Weidner, has been described as a wonderful, caring, sharing person. Some have said he would loan you anything and even give you the shirt off his back. Many people described him as being very friendly and quite talkative. Mother did tell me once that she worried about Abe and his generosity. She indicated he had a lack of desire for material things and always wanted to help others.

Looking back into Abe's family tree gives us a glimpse of his German/Russian heritage. Abe's mother's family traveled from the Necker River Region near Waiblingen, Germany (in the vicinity of Stuttgart, Germany) and settled in the Rosenfeld, Hannovka area of Russia. It was in October 1895, that Matilda Schaefer (my grandma) was born in Orangeburg, Russia. She came to America sometime in June or July 1913, and was about 17 1/2 years old. Arriving on Ellis Island, she was able to get to Wisconsin, where she had some connections. It was thought she knew the Weidners and had done some housecleaning for them while living in Racine, Wisconsin. There she met Louis Weidner, and married him sometime after. In the fall of 1916, they moved to Tangier, Oklahoma with Abraham Weidner and there she gave birth to another son, Leo.

Louie's father, John, and his mother Luisa, along with 7 other kids, also moved to Oklahoma. Several of John's children later moved to South Dakota and settled in different parts of the state. Places some settled were Delmont, Cologne, Winner, Fairfax and Bonesteel. The Fairfax graveyard has many Weidner tombstones.

Ludwig, also known as Louie, and Matilda settled in the Delmont area where three more children were born. Sometime between the last child born in South Dakota and the next which was born in 1923 they resettled in Racine, Wisconsin. Hard times in South Dakota drove them to seek factory jobs in the city. Of the eight children born to Ludwig and Matilda only one left and returned to South Dakota, and that was Abraham. Abraham was a young boy when they moved from Delmont back to Wisconsin. Sometime during 1925 the last child was born to that family.

While living in Delmont, Abe may have learned to love the area and that's why he felt a desire to come back to South Dakota. One of the people he later met was my mother's brother, George M. Hofer, from Bridgewater. They ran the rail lines in search of work in 1933 and 1934. Their travels led them to Kansas, Minnesota and North Dakota. While George and Abe were searching for work, my mother was going to Freeman Junior College and staying at the John L. Hofer farm for room and board. Apparently, John L. Hofer needed help, so mother informed George of a job opening on the farm. It just so happened that George liked one of the John L. Hofer girls. Mother agreed to set up a date with George if he would get her a date with his friend Abe Weidner. Both dates turned out okay and both couples were eventually married.

Mother finished her schooling and returned to Beadle County to seek a teaching job, which she did get at Ackerman School northwest of Yale. Abe followed her to the area to continue courting mother and they were married in October 1936. Four children were born to this couple in the next seven years, until tragedy struck in 1943.

Looking back at some of the old photos of Abe, we soon discovered just how tall he was. No mention was ever made of his height, but when my grandson began to grow tall and eventually reached 6'5", we started wondering where the height in the family came from. We now believe that my dad was at least that tall judging by some of the photos we have discovered.

Meeting his untimely death at age 29 prevented our entire family from ever developing a family unit. Mother was cast into a role she neither wanted nor felt qualified to fulfill. Carrying on she must in spite of sorrow, pain and total feelings of helplessness. I have been haunted my whole life wondering how things might have been if we could've stayed a complete family unit. Only God knows the goodness He intended to come out of such pain, hurt and confusion.

Where was God?

No one could ever give me the assurance that my father will be in heaven when I get there. Yes, people could say he was baptized and confirmed into the church. But were they just words spoken to meet the requirements for membership, as I had spoken mine, or did he have a real heart change when and if he asked Christ into his life? There is no doubt in my mind that he certainly lived a compassionate life and cared for others. I so want to believe that those feelings came from his desire to share with others the real source, which was his love for Jesus. How can any of us experience real joy in heaven if both our parents aren't there to enjoy it with us? Some things cannot be answered, but this I know: God's love and His plans are perfect. God was there through all of this turmoil, He is here today and He wants us to trust in Him no matter how unclear the past is or how cloudy the future might look. When I have come to the end of my human reasoning, the only thing left is trust. It is so easy for us to tell our children to just trust us, we know what's best. Does our heavenly father have any less concern for us than we do for our children? The words of an old hymn come to mind... "trust and obey, for there's no other way."

Mother and Father

3

Memories You Can't Out Run

Because of the shock and trauma my mother went through that awful day, she shut the door to her past life and it was forever closed. As I reflect on my own life, and the challenges I have gone through, they seem pale to what happened that day. My mother lost the love of her life in a split second and all her hopes and dreams were forever shattered. It is incomprehensible, and I can only imagine her feeling of hopelessness was closing in all-around. There were no answers to her questions of where do we go now with no home, no car and no money.

For some reason, none of us can answer the question why the subject of his death never came up again. Why we never inquired about that day or anything in our past is a mystery. Mother took to her grave the key that might have unlocked the door to all our questions. Maybe we realized that a Pandora's Box might have been opened to a lot of old hurts and scars that she carried to her grave. I believe that a part of my mother died that day and she never wanted to go back to that time and place. Perhaps each of us is now trying to survive the trauma in our own way and in our own silence.

I know that mother shed many tears after the loss of her husband. It was in her tears that she drifted off to sleep for weeks on end. It must've been easier to box up all her feelings and throw them in a place and shut the door to hopefully never open again. Songwriters and artists who sing are so gifted in the words they put on paper. This past year has been a year when I have listened with what I learned in my counseling program what Carl Rogers called the "third ear." What did the songwriter mean by his words, and how did the singer project that feeling? A musical group I have come to love called "Home Free" sang a Trace Adkins' song he wrote called, "I can't outrun you." I have printed it here for you because I believe that the song represents what mother was going through. It may have haunted her until she left this earth. Read the words and imagine my mother thinking about the love of her life that she lost way too soon. How can any of us outrun a memory so powerful that it is in my heart, in my mind, everywhere ahead and everywhere behind. Every turn I take you're right around the bend; your ghost chases me when I'm asleep and when I'm awake. I can't outrun you.

"I can't outrun you" by Trace Atkins

95 down the interstate
Mile high on a jet plane
Desert road or a downtown train
It's all the same
I can't outrun you
Now I can move to another town
And nobody to ask where you are now
LA or Mexico
No matter where I go
I can't outrun you
You're in my heart
You're in my mind
Everywhere ahead

Everywhere behind
Every turn I take
You're right around the bend
It's like your ghost is chasing me
When I'm awake
When I'm asleep
There's a part of you in every part of me
And I can't outrun you
I can't outrun you
Now I've had a chance with a girl (guy) or two
But all I ever saw was you
Holding my hand
Kiss in my face
I guess some pictures never fade
You're in my heart
You are in my mind
Everywhere ahead
Everywhere behind
Every turn I take
You're right around the bend
It's like your post is chasing me
When I'm wake
When I'm asleep
There's a part of you
In every part of me
I can't outrun you. No.
I can't outrun you. No.
I can't outrun
Though there might just come a time
We regret telling you goodbye
But looking back
Should I realized

I can't outrun you
I can't outrun you
I can't outrun you

This song is about a lost love of a girl, but I imagine this happening to my mother as she thought about her loss. How does a person let go of a love for a lost husband when every day you are reminded of that love by the movement of the child you carry within. This child is a part of both of you.

Can a broken heart be mended and hurts healed? True healing comes as Jesus said in Matthew 11:28-30. "Come unto me, all ye that labor and are heavy laden, and I will give you rest. Take my yoke upon you and learn of me, for I am meek and lowly in heart; and you shall find rest unto your souls. For my yoke is easy, and my burden is light."

Where was God?

The reality of life is that when going through really tough times, it is hard to look at the big picture as God sees it. We do not always see the good while we are in the eye of the storm. As a much wiser, older person, I can now look over each struggle and see God's hand at work. Warren Wiersbe says, "When God permits his children to go through the furnace; He keeps his eye on the temperature and His hand on the thermostat."

As long as I can remember, my mother never questioned God. There never was a time that bitterness and anger showed through in her words or actions. Even though my mother wasn't one who spoke about her personal faith, I know that her upbringing was deep in a conservative, Mennonite heritage. More will be said about mother and her life as I devote a complete chapter to her.

4

A Sign of His Presence

After the death of my father, one particular story continued to crop up. I wanted very much to believe this story, and it was recently confirmed by a neighbor who was actually there. At the end of the day before my father was killed, some of the men finished the day by parking the hayrack in the field and sticking their forks in the ground. Others laid their forks on the side of the rack. When the men arrived to start thrashing that next day, they discovered Abe's fork handle was split from top to bottom. Many would say it was a mere coincidence, but as I reflect on God, I believe He was sending a signal to us, showing us that our father's work on earth was finished, and that God was there that day. That fork says to me that He was present then and He will never leave us alone. We just need to call on Him. He will walk with us through life no matter how difficult life can get. This sign says to me, "I will help you navigate your way through rough waters of life, in spite of your terrible loss." Hebrews 13:5 reminds us, "I will never leave thee nor forsake." John 14:18 says, "I will never leave you comfortless. I will come to you." Romans 8:28 explains, "we know that all things work together for good to them that love God, to them who are called according to his purpose."

There are many reasons God may allow us to suffer. God wants us to use trials to bring glory unto Himself, and help us to see how God has led and worked in our lives. Maybe he wants some of us to be like the one-way missionaries who packed their belongings in coffins to travel to islands were cannibals and headhunters lived. One such man was A. W. Milne, who set sail for New Hebrides in the South Pacific Island in the early 1800's. He knew that other missionaries had lost their lives to headhunters and cannibals there. He packed his coffin and left, knowing that was the only way he would come home. How could he go? He had already died to self. As Galatians 2:20 says, "I am crucified with Christ, nevertheless I live yet not I but Christ lives within me." After 35 years on the island, he had converted the whole island, except one demented native who eventually killed him. The converted natives buried him in the center of the city with this epitaph on his tombstone:

> When he came there was no light.
> When he left there was no darkness.

When did we start believing that God wants to send us to safe places to do easy things or never to suffer tragedies? When did we start believing that faithfulness is holding the fort and that playing it safe is safe? When did we start believing that Jesus didn't die to make us safe? He died to make us dangerous. Matthew 10:34. When did we start believing faithfulness is not holding the fort, it's storming the gates of hell. When did we start believing in it's time to quit living as if the purpose of life is to arrive safely at death. Mark Batterson – "All In"

From this sign God is saying to me "shed your light wherever life leads you. Try to help someone who lives in darkness. Sow some seeds of faith and hope, even if it is small as a mustard seed. We never know who we touch that might just light a candle in their life just as others have lit candles in our lives."

Where was God?

I realize that I cannot know for sure the meaning behind this incident. Does it not seem strange that out of all the pitchforks in the field that only my dad's fork was hit? Did the same lightning strike hit my dad and his fork, or what are the chances of two strikes hitting so close together?

We look back, not to question God, but rather to look at ways God works in and through circumstances to show his presence and his power. My faith is strengthened as I look at my 20 years before Christ and 55+ years after Christ. I hope to share how he led in each phase of my life.

Farm Sale

FARM AUCTION

Evening Huron H& *Friday Sept 3, 1943*

Due to the death of my husband I will sell at public auction on the Jim Chapman farm on the SE ¼ of Sec. 29-112-60; 6 miles north, 8 east, 1½ north of Huron; 7½ miles north, 1 west of Cavour; 1½ miles north, 4 west; 1½ north of Yale, on

Tuesday, Sept. 7, 1943

Sale Starts at 1:30 pm. Central War Time

2--HORSES--2	13--CATTLE--13
1 sorrel mare, 4 yrs., 1500 1 sorrel gelding, 4 yrs., 1500	1 Guernsey cow, 2 yrs. 1 roan cow, 8 yrs. 3 Holstein cows, 4-5 yrs.
31--HOGS--31	1 Guernsey Heifer, spring, 2 yrs. 1 black heifer, springing, 2 yrs.
4 Sows 20 spring pigs 7 fall pigs	(These are very good milk cows) 1 roan bull, 2 yrs. 2 white face steers, 8 months 1 black white face steer, 8 mo.
15--SHEEP--15	2 Holstein calves, 2 mo.
12 ewes, 3-4 yrs. 5 ewe lambs	**200 PULLETS—AAA-4A**

MACHINERY
1939 Farmall Tractor, F-20, on rubber, very good condition; new Co-Op Cream Separator; 2-bottom tractor plow; 2 row cultivator; 8-ft. disc; wagon box; hayrack; new set harness and collars; other articles too numerous to mention.

TERMS: Cash or see your banker before sale. All items must be settled for day of sale.

Mrs. Abraham Weidner

Ron Weidner's Mother

Roy Housman, Auctioneer

Farmers & Merchants Bank, Huron Clerk

5

Choices in Tragedy

Tragedy comes to all of us. It comes in different forms and intensities. It seems like we have either just passed one, are presently in one, or one is just over the horizon. Are we prepared for the worst to happen or do we go through life hoping to dodge its difficulties? Both the number and intensities of tragedies will certainly vary with each one of us. As humans we do have free well. Free will means we have many choices to make when confronted with life's problems. We can get bitter or we can get better. We can panic or we can pray.

Given the circumstances and options available to my mother and family, I am amazed how well each of us came through this tragedy. Even later trials in life were met with grace and dignity. It would have been easy for any member to use this as an excuse to justify a lifestyle of bitterness and hatred. There was never a time in my memory that anyone ever used this tragedy as an excuse for bad behavior or to justify a questionable lifestyle.

Hurt feelings are like fertilizer to bitterness and make it grow like a weed. Bitterness is like a root that grows deep in the soil of our heart and soul. If watered with resentment and anger, it often raises its ugly head like a Jack-in-the-Box. Bitterness and anger has a way of multiplying and it becomes a nagging, sour and hateful habit. Ephesians 4:31

reminds us to "let all bitterness and wrath and anger and clamor and evil speaking be put away from you with all malice."

My soul needs weeding sometimes but I know the gardener who can cleanse me by pulling out the roots of bitterness. There are two kinds of wells we eventually drink from, and they will determine the kind of life we will live.

A. Well of bitterness.

The world is quick to question why bad things happen and ask where God was. If we allow ourselves to drink from the world's well of bitterness, it will only produce more anger and more disappointment. This will probably manifest itself by us shaking our fist at God and blaming Him for everything. If we continue to drink from this well, it will permeate every part of our being. Eventually it will destroy any happiness.

I am grateful for being raised in a somewhat dysfunctional family that never spoke of any bitterness. There was never a time when we questioned God or felt sorry for ourselves. Looking back, we didn't have time to be bitter. Our lives were filled with work and school. Mother and stepdad really set the tone in our household. Both of them had experienced unwanted tragedy but rose above self-pity and sorrow to live meaningful lives. Hebrews 12:14–15 tells us to "follow peace with all men, and holiness, without which no man shall see the Lord; looking diligently lest any man fail of the grace of God; lest any root of bitterness spring up trouble you, and thereby many be defiled."

B. Well of Living Water

There is another well that we can drink from if we choose. The weeping prophet Jeremiah says in Chapter 2:13, "for my people have committed two evils; they have forsaken me the fountain of living waters." Jeremiah was warning Judah (the southern kingdom) of what was to happen because they had turned away from their God. They were failing in their desire to fill themselves with the thirst-quenching Word of God. No longer were the rituals, customs and commands of God being followed. Doom was pronounced on Judah in the days ahead. The northern kingdom had already fallen to the Assyrians in 721, and they were after Judah. Were it not for a godly King Hezekiah, who prayed for Jerusalem, and 185,000 Assyrians were killed, the city would have fallen. By prayers of one godly man, a city was saved. This lasted only for a while, until 586 when the Babylonians did capture the city.

How many of us have experienced real thirst for physical water and found it? I have tasted the water that runs out of mountain springs. Both the Kasilof and the Kenai Rivers in Alaska produce cold, clear, sweet and very satisfying water. That's the kind of satisfaction Jeremiah is talking about, but his people fail to go to that fountain. John says in Revelations 22:1 "and he showed me a pure river water of life clear as crystal proceeding out of the throne of God and of the way." Revelations 22:17b says "Let the one who is thirsty come; and let the one who wishes take the free gift of the water of life."

These verses tell us when tragedies come, our soul thirsts for comfort and God's Word is the only source that satisfies our deepest longings. Oh, that we could be like the psalmist in 63:1 who cries out, "my soul thirsts for thee, my flesh longs for thee in a dry and thirsty land."

In the second part of this verse 2:13, Jeremiah gives us a great analog, and he hewed them out cisterns, broken cisterns, that can hold no water. I remember going to my grandparents' home and pumping water from their cistern. There were times when it was dry because no rain fell. Cisterns were close to the house and water from the roof ran in to fill the cistern. Jeremiah is asking why people would build cisterns that will not hold water. If a cistern is to be helpful in dry times, it must have water in it. I think he was saying they were putting their faith in things they considered more precious than even water. But when tough times come, there will be nothing there. What are you and I putting our trust and faith in to carry us through the tough times? Is your security in your bank balance, 401K's, pension plan, good name, position in your community, cars, boats, spouse etc.. What will keep you in tough times? Unless your cistern is full of faith, the world has no hope to offer you. Faith comes by hearing God's Word and He will take us through the speed bumps in life. Fill your cistern with faith and you can then draw from that faith when needed. I ask you not what's in your wallet, but what's in your cistern? Just as our bodies cry out for water, so does our soul.

We need cisterns not only for our physical bodies but also for our spiritual bodies. One holds water and the other holds faith. Just like the cisterns of old that were filled by rain falling from above and running off the roofs. The filling of our spiritual cisterns comes from above in the form of trials. Through all my years of suffering, I have learned the reason God might call you to suffer as listed in another chapter. My cistern runneth over, what about yours?

Where was God?

Even though we might make bad choices during or after a tragedy, that doesn't mean God can't use us later in life. Scripture gives us many examples of people who did great things later in life:

Jacob was a cheater
Peter had a temper
David had an affair
Noah was a drunk
Jonah ran from God
Paul was a murderer
Gideon was insecure
Mariam was a gossiper
Martha was a worrier
Thomas was a doubter
Sarah was impatient
Elijah was moody
Mary Magdalene was a hooker
Moses stuttered
Zacchaeus was short
Abraham was old
Lazarus was dead

God doesn't call the qualified he qualifies the called. God used these heroes of old, even though they had trials and failures. Don't you think God wants to use you and me to tell our story of love, forgiveness and restoration to his fellowship?

6

Conceived in Love/ Born in Tragedy

Knowing nothing about your father is a terrible thing. What kind of person was he? Did he love kids? Do you enjoy playing with them? Were they hoping and planning for at least one more child? When they found out I was coming, was there as much excitement as the other children? Never being able to answer that question, I choose to assume they planned and were excited about another child. I can't help wondering what people were saying about me after I was born. Does he look like his dad or his mom? Will he get tall like his dad? What about his mother's dark hair? As a parent, grandparent, and now great grandparent, I wonder how much of my dad is being passed on to each generation. There's a song sung by Home Free, written by John Mayer, called "In the Blood." The words keep ringing in my mind and asking this question:

IN THE BLOOD

> How much of my mother has my mother left in me?
> How much of my love will be insane to some degree?
> And what about this feeling that I'm never good enough? Will it wash out in the water or is it always in the blood?

How much of my father am I destined to become? Will it dim the lights inside me just to satisfy someone? Will I let this woman kill me, or do away with jealous love? Will it wash out in the water, or is it always in the blood?

I can feel the love I want, I can feel the love I need. But it's never going to come the way I am. Could I change it if I wanted, cannot rise above the flood? Will it wash out in the water, or is it always in the blood?

How much like my brothers, do my brothers wanna be? Does a broken home become another broken family? Or will we be there for each other, like nobody ever could? Will it wash out in the water, or is it always in the blood?

I can feel the love I want, I can feel the love I need but it's never going to come the way I am. Could I change it if I wanted, could I rise above the flood? Will it wash out in the water or is it always in the blood?

Can I feel the love I want, I can feel the love I need but it's never going to come the way I am. Can I change it if I wanted, can I rise above the flood? Will it wash out in the water, or is it always in the blood?

Because of the nature of our mother and her inability to share anything about her past, many questions I had remained unanswered. At this point, I take some literary license to assume the truth in the title of this section. It would serve no purpose to assume any other thought. I have found great consolation in Jeremiah 1:5 that says: "before I formed thee in the belly I knew thee: and before thou camest forth out of the womb I sanctified thee." I understand that the Lord is telling this to Jeremiah, but he would say nothing less to each and every child. It says in Psalms 139:13-16, "for thou hast possessed my reins: thou hast covered me in my mother's womb. I will praise thee: for I am fearfully and wonderfully made: marvelous are thy works; and that my soul knoweth right well. My substance was not hid from thee, when I was made in secret and curiously wrought in the lowest parts of the earth. Thine eyes did not see my subsidence, yet being imperfect: and in thy book all my members were written, which in continuance were fashioned, when as yet there was none of them." Ephesians 1:4 says, "according as he had chosen us in him before the foundation of the world, that we should be holy and without blame before him in love."

Stop and think that the great I am knew each of us before the foundation of the world! He had a plan to call each one of us unto himself because of what Christ did on the cross. Can we now not bear any cross, endure any pain, suffer all tragedies and even die to self to return our love to him who we owe so much?

One of the great luxuries of having both parents there at the birth of a child is the ability to experience confirmation of their joy and love. It was only 71 days from my father's death to my birth. Somehow a choice was made that this family needed another child to be complete. Unfortunately, life does not always work out like we planned. A mother with three children is about to bring another into this world. This world filled with confusion, doubt, hopelessness, despair and where no answers seem to be found.

Where was God?

We need only to look to Scripture just quoted to see that God knew each of us before the foundation of the world. Ours is not to question why each of us were born, but rather, what can I do with my life to fulfill God's purpose through my life?

> Christ came to earth to become like us,
> so that we might become like him.

University, Syracuse, N. Y.

A son, weighing eight pounds, was born to Mrs. Abe Weidner of Yale at 10 a. m. Wednesday, Oct. 20, in a Huron hospital. Mr. Weidner lost his life when struck by lightning while working on his farm in Liberty Township early the morning of Aug. 10.

During the first half of 1943

7

From Death Pains to Birth Pains

My heart aches as I ponder the dilemma mother faced as she tried to get over the lost love of her life. His memory was everywhere and she couldn't outrun the feeling of loss. I'm sure that was true as she tried to cope with the loss of the love of her life. The joy, love, anticipation and dreams that they shared resurfaced with every move of the child she carried within her. The result of that love was now a part of her. I am convinced that as I look back over her life, I believe a part of her died with my dad. Every decision she made afterwards seemed to be with little emotion or feeling. She moved forward and did whatever she had to for survival.

Within the last year, my aunt who had taken care of us as kids told me of the emotional agony my mother went through. She cried herself to sleep every night for six weeks. Having to move back home with her folks with her three children must have been very humiliating. I'm sure that she was torn between grieving for the past, trying to cope with the present, and looking forward to answers for her family's future.

Experiencing the loss of her husband and all the pain involved soon gave way to a new kind of pain…that being the pain of birth. Never having experienced the pains of birth, it's hard for me to go there emotionally. I have been told by a few women that have experienced both birth and kidney stone pains they are very close. One of my many medical speed bumps in life has been kidney stones. I do know the depth of that pain and do not care to ever experience that again.

I later learned some feared I may be stillborn. Adoption was also brought up, as a couple from Freeman, South Dakota was seeking to adopt because they were childless. I can only imagine the day of my birth was a bittersweet day. How can the pain of death be diminished by the birth of a child? I couldn't help wondering what the ramifications of prolonged stress might be on the fetus. Research shows extreme stress during pregnancy can cause physical, mental and or psychological damage to the fetus. I was lucky to not be born with any visible physical abnormalities. There are some family members and maybe others who feel the jury is still out on the mental and psychological abnormalities.

Where was God?

My mother must have received some kind of special inner strength. For her to switch from the deepest kind of pain one could feel to what would normally be the greatest joy must have been humanly impossible. Not knowing anything of her emotional state after my birth, I can only imagine her having mixed feelings at the time. Was she grateful that she gave birth to a healthy son? Did she find any joy looking at her son and seeing a part of her lost husband? Growing up did she look at this child and often think that he acts just like his father?

I believe there must have been hundreds of prayers that went up for my mother in this terrible hour. Several people who lived during this time have shared with me how much the whole community was moved with compassion towards my family. If I could, I would now ask mother what carried her through this tragedy. I believe faith, family and friends would be her answer. She would often tell us you have to be tough in life. She was one tough lady.

8

Pool Halls Plus Swearing Equals Orange Pop

It was only 50 days after the death of my father that my mom's older sister and her husband stepped forward and purchased a home in Yale for our family. This house was one block west of the restaurant on Main Street. It was 21 days later that I was born into this world. After staying at my grandfather's home for some time, we moved into our new home in Yale. I have few memories of those early days, since I was just a baby. The house had two bedrooms. My two older brothers and sister slept together in one room, while mom slept in the other room along with my crib. My earliest memory is waking up in the crib with gum all over the crib and in my hair. I remember mom getting the scissors and cutting my hair to get the gum out. Someone must've had to settle with mom for giving me gum before bedtime.

As I became more mobile, my outings became more frequent and over a greater distance. Years later I was told that quite often I escaped from our yard, crossed the alley, and climbed a long series of wooden steps to see a girl I apparently liked a lot. Adina Hohm was probably in high school and I was only one or two at the time. Mother had made some kind of an arrangement with her younger sister to watch over the four kids while she did waitress work at the local restaurant. This sister was only 14 at the time and I'm sure she had a lot of things on her mind besides babysitting. It would be impossible to keep track of all four of us since we were used to roaming all over town.

Surely God was watching over all of us during this time. My aunt recently shared two stories about her taking care of me. Once she had me lying in the front seat of the car she was riding in. Someone suddenly opened that door and I rolled off the seat and landed on the road. A second incident happened when she was asked by her folks to go to town to get a bag of potatoes. I must've been at the farm with her and begged to go along. On the way home, my aunt said I told her she was a crazy driver and going too fast. Shortly after that remark, she crossed over a large ridge of gravel in the middle of the road, loss control, hit the ditch and rolled over. Folks who were following her were there to help her out of the car and asked how she felt. Her first response was, "where are the potatoes?" Their response didn't include the potatoes, but they did ask about the little boy lying in the weeds in the ditch! Over the years we both laughed about how she tried, on two occasions, to do away with me. She was not successful since I was unhurt both times.

I have no idea what my brothers and sisters were up to during our five years there. I am sure we were all given wide latitude to roam free. There is one story I find hard to believe, but it was later told to me. It was about the time I bit another girl on the arm. I then ran home and hid under the bed for a long time.

Since mother was working for $0.28 an hour, there certainly wasn't money for any kind of toys, but somehow I ended up with a scooter. This was a two-wheeled toy with a platform between the wheels where you can stand on and push with the other foot. It also had handlebars to steer with. After days of riding up and down the sidewalk, the local postmaster began to call me "the scooter man." I don't remember why or when, but he later called me "Superman".

Riding my scooter each day usually put me in the area of the local pool hall. Being young and looking for attention, I spent a lot of time just hanging around. My favorite spot was sitting on one of the high chairs in the southeast corner of the pool hall. From there I could look outside and watch men playing cards, mixing drinks, spitting in the spittoon and even swearing now and then. My vocabulary grew by leaps and bounds, depending on how the card game was going. I suppose there were times I became a real pest to the guys and they would tease me. My response was usually to respond back in the same language they were using. Yes, I learned to swear at a very early age, and it made the men laugh. Some of the kindhearted men must have felt sorry for this little boy with no father and offered to buy me a bottle of orange pop. Even at a young age, I figured out what I needed to do if I wanted a bottle of orange pop. Yes, just make myself a pest, get teased, swear just a little and someone would come through and feel sorry for me with another bottle of orange pop.

When I was a little older I was able to attend the local co-op annual meetings. I was in my glory. As a kid we used to see who could drink the most pop since it was free in tubs all over the building. I remember the night I drank seven bottles of orange. Some of these bottles I downed without stopping at all. My sister claims my skin actually turned orange after a while.

Where was God?

While there were no social safety nets available for my mother, I often wondered how we survived with her wages at $0.28 an hour. A person might even wonder where God was. Mother told me that the hearts of people were moved in hundreds of ways. God used people with tender loving hearts, moved by compassion at the tragedy mother faced. Tips were sometimes as much as a meal. People would often stop by the house and leave various amounts of money. Many times food was also left at the house. Never once did I remember going hungry. What all was God doing during this time? Well, He was working in the hearts of a sister and brother-in-law to buy a house. He provided a waitress job and ironing work. He was moving in the hearts of many people in the community. All the while, He was providing free babysitting services. Most importantly, He was protecting the whole family from harm. What a day that will be for me as I witness Jesus rewarding all those who gave and shared in Jesus' name for helping my family through really tough times. I will know each and every person that made a sacrifice on our behalf and will love spending eternity thanking each of them.

9

Broken Hearts Merge

Living only 6 miles apart, two couples began their married lives with similar hopes and dreams. My parents' marriage began in October 1936, and my step-dad married his first wife in January 1937. Abe and Edna (my parents) were married six years and nine months before my father's death. My stepdad, Mark Davis, and his wife Izetta, were married one year and four months before her untimely death.

Ten months after their wedding, a son was born to Mark and Izetta Davis on November 12, 1937. Izetta got to see and hold her son for six months and eleven days before she died at the age of 26 from complications arising from childbirth. Unable to take care of this new son, Mark allowed a sister and her husband to raise him. As the boy was growing up, I don't have any knowledge of the kind of relationship, if any, he had with his father. I can easily identify with feelings he must have had growing up, because he, in reality, lost both parents.

Mother was a waitress at the Yale café and this farmer who had lost his wife often came to town and ate at the restaurant. The first meeting between Mark and my mother was when mother and others got stuck on a dirt road somewhere between grandma and grandpa's home and the Mark Davis farm, which was two a half miles north. Mr. Davis came along and pulled them out of the mud with his horses.

Somehow out of their brokenness, they found a way to get past the hurt and sorrow and allowed their broken hearts to merge. None of us have any knowledge of their dating or proposals of marriage, but they were married on September 26, 1948. Over the 24 years and four 1/2 months of their marriage, I never witnessed affection of any kind between my mother and stepdad. I'm assuming the generation they both grew up in was very reserved and didn't believe in publicly showing any affection. In all my growing up years, both in town and then on the farm, the words "I love you" were never heard. Deep down inside I can't help feeling that mother made this marriage decision based on the needs of her four children. Regardless of her motives, I saw her determination to make this marriage work in spite of his alcoholism and lack of financial accountability. Mother was a strong person and got her husband into AA and also took over the checkbook. My stepdad was quite cooperative with all of this and allowed her to take charge. After several years of AA, things got a lot better with fewer weekend binges. Being a man of few words most of the time, I know how grateful he was for having clean clothes, a clean house and fantastic meals. Mother was not particularly happy about her husband's smoking habit, but conceded this one point knowing she probably was not going to win that battle. Looking back, I think it was good, because none of us now smoke. We got tired of living in a smoke-filled house because he was a very heavy smoker rolling his own for many years.

A big surprise came our way about 2 1/2 years into the marriage when mother said she had to go to the hospital. A few days later, she came home and seemed quite well. Some of us found out what happened when mother was asked about a baby in the grocery store. There wasn't the slightest knowledge on my part that mother was pregnant, had a baby, and the baby was stillborn. We later learned that the cord was wrapped around his neck. I would have been about 7 1/2 at the time. There wasn't even a hint on my part of what was happening since I knew nothing about having babies or anything related. My brothers had supplied me with false information regarding babies. Their explanation was that cows would cough up the baby to give birth. Imagine my surprise and big eyes looking through a hole in the door when I saw my first calf actually being born. Ever since that time I question my brother's truthfulness. My half-brother Michael Edward Davis was stillborn on May 16, 1951 in St. John's Hospital. He is buried beside his dad in St. William Cemetery just a few miles from where we grew up.

Where was God?

I am grateful the way God led these two people to meet. Yes, these were two dysfunctional families that came together. Getting beyond the raw emotions of lost love must have been bittersweet. Driven by reality, they each made a commitment to move past hurts and sorrow to build a new life together. Maybe it wasn't their ideal choice in life, but both grabbed onto this new life. I know that my mother made every effort to make the best of the situation. In Mark's eulogy I wrote the following "with this marriage he took on the immediate and awesome responsibility of providing for a family of seven. Four boys and one girl proved to be a real challenge during the growing up years. Each of us will never forget the fights, the hardships and above all else the unselfish commitment he had in providing for our needs. Words cannot express that which we feel about his providing for our educational opportunities. Our lives have indeed been enriched by his sharing. In these times of high mobility, crumbling family structures and a lack of home base for many people, we are indeed grateful for having had a place to call home. By his life Mark taught us all the meaning of work, the richness of life to be found in the land and by his daily devotion to God the strength to meet the trials of life. How appropriate and fitting that God in his wisdom has seen fit that Mark should be laid to rest on the land he loved so much."

Mother and Stepdad

10

Theological Ideologies Clash

We are told that there are two things to avoid if you want to prevent an argument: religion and politics. Since there were no premarital counseling classes in those days, there were some things that were not dealt with right away. My stepdad was Roman Catholic and had strong ideas on how some things should be done, including the idea that one must be married in the Catholic Church.

Mother's early childhood upbringing in Freeman, South Dakota was in the Mennonite tradition, but after her first marriage to Abraham Weidner, she was confirmed and baptized into St. John's Evangelical Lutheran congregation in Racine, Wisconsin on March 8, 1942. Their marriage had taken place at Trinity Lutheran Church in Yale, South Dakota on October 25, 1936 several years earlier. During my parent's visit to Racine, Wisconsin, pressure was put on my dad that mother was not a true Lutheran until confirmed and baptized. Mother agreed to do this to keep peace in the family. All three children were already baptized in the Lutheran Church at Yale.

Anyone with any knowledge about Lutheranism and Catholicism realize they are not exactly close in their interpretation of church doctrine. Mother agreed to be married by the priest at Cavour, South Dakota on September 26, 1948. Rather than make religion a big issue in the marriage, both agreed to each go their own way. Even though all four of us kids were confirmed in the Yale Lutheran church, there were a few years in my early days that I found myself going to church with my stepdad. I think he kind of liked it when I went through some of the motions he went through, including saying the rosary. After all these years, I have not forgotten the words. I readily confess my intent was far from spiritual. The church had some good looking girls and there was roller skating in the church basement several times during the year. I loved the social aspects of going to church. For years, I would attend the church's annual grave yard cleanup day just for the joy of serving alongside cute girls. I was the only child that spent a lot of time with my stepdad at the Catholic Church. All of my brothers and sisters went with mother most of the time. I did take part in most of the Christmas programs in Yale. Eventually, all of us ended up going through the classes to be confirmed into the church because all of us were baptized as children. I had a problem with attendance and was in danger of not getting confirmed unless I made up some classes. I caved in and went two or three extra Saturdays so I would make it with my age group. Even though I learned what I needed to about the church's doctrine and position on different issues, nothing ever stirred my heart. I find no fault in the church but only in myself. Unless a person's heart is open and receptive to the calling of the Holy Spirit, there is no help anywhere. Later on in high school, I thought I found some justification for my resistance to the church when we were told not to go to baccalaureate because there would be other faiths there and that would not be good for us. As I recall all four of us seniors from the church did go ahead and attend in spite of the pastor's plea not to go.

Where was God?

During all those years of growing up and searching to find myself, God was not one of the things I was looking for. When your life is governed by the feelings of being lost, lonely and loveless, these are the driving forces in your life. I believe that the Holy Spirit can work in and through many denominations when hearts are open to His teaching. I was never boldly confronted by anyone with the inward passion of the Gospel message. Several of my classmates in school were very dedicated church goers and lived lives that amplified their inner beliefs. Growing up, I never looked at anyone and said that I wanted what they had. The dualisms that bombarded my life and thoughts only kept me from seeking the true source of peace and contentment. Being baptized as a child and also confirmed into the church at Yale seem to have minimal affect on my life. I place no blame either with the Lutheran or the Catholic churches. The mere fact that their teaching did not seem to alter my lifestyle is only a reflection of my own unwillingness to change and not the fault of either church. We only change when we are ready and willing to make such changes. For me, that change didn't happen until later in life.

11

A Stranger Among Us

Sometime during the late fall 1948 or in the spring of 1949, our family grew by one more. Our step-dad decided to bring his son Jerry home to live with us. None of us ever knew the reason why this happened. The family he lived with was getting quite large and perhaps he was getting to be a burden on them. Perhaps he belonged with us to complete these two dysfunctional families. Since I was the youngest child, I had less of a problem adjusting to our new stepbrother. As far back as I can remember, he had a real angry, resentful, "I don't care" attitude. This would manifest itself by how he treated mother by not obeying her. Even his dad had trouble keeping him in line. I have always felt sorry for him because of losing his mother and never having someone to bond with and show him real love. It seemed like he resisted authority in everything. When it came to helping milk 15-17 cows morning and night, my brothers could milk five to his one. Since I operated the separator, I often found chunks of manure in the pail where a cow put her foot in the pail. After a while, I just fed his milk to the pail calves. For years we left a little milk in the glass because we often saw dirt at the bottom. No matter what kind of work we did, he always managed to have a poor attitude.

A real conflict occurred when my brothers bought a very nice car. They bought it with the money that was left from our farm sale. In reality, it belonged to my brothers but our stepdad said his son could drive it on one occasion. Things were never good after we learned he had wrecked the car in an accident.

Our home only had two bedrooms downstairs and a cold attic upstairs. Mother and our stepdad had one downstairs bedroom and our sister had the other. For a few years I shared a room with my sister but eventually all four of us boys slept in the attic. My brothers slept together in one bad and I was stuck with my stepbrother in the other. We cooked in the summer and froze in the winter. The only heat came from the chimney and the open door up the stairs. Many times we woke up in winter with snow on our beds. The room itself was about 20'X16' with 2 foot high sidewalls and barely sloped to 6 foot in the center where we walked. We were lucky because our room had windows on each end. The east window was just above our folks' bedroom roof and many times when we were too cold to go outside to use the outhouse, the window served that purpose. After about a year my mother could not figure out why that corner of the house smelled so bad. Well the truth always has a way of surfacing and it did. So much for our well hidden "indoor" bathroom.

Apparently the rules and work proved too much for my stepbrother, so he found a place to live and work and then left home. This happened sometime in his junior year of high school in 1955 and he never moved home again. Right after graduation, he joined the Army and took his six weeks basic training somewhere in Texas. Upon arriving in Sioux Falls after training, he met the farmer's daughter where he worked, and off they went to Pipestone, Minnesota to get married. He was then ordered to Annapolis, Maryland to finish his service. Because of his drinking and lifestyle, the marriage ended in two years. Once out of the service he got a job as a pile driver on road construction in Richmond, Va. He remarried again to a woman who had several children by a previous marriage. She was somewhat older than he was but they stayed together until her death.

Through the years he would occasionally return home, especially during school reunions. I always tried to have a good rapport with him because I still felt sorry for him. I know we all have choices in life. If he ever needed someone, I wanted to be there for him. During one of his trips home he saw a car that he just had to have. He knew that his grandpa had put a quarter of land in his name and he wanted enough money out of it to buy that car. His dad said he would give him the money to get that car if he'd sign over that quarter of land to him. Everyone agreed, so he got his car but lost the quarter of land. When he drove in the yard with his car I knew why he had to have that car. It was a 1956 crown Victoria Ford painted black, white and yellow on the outside and had black and white checkered seats inside. It had a 12 inch chrome strip that ran up one side across roof and down the other. It was the prettiest car I had ever seen. It didn't take very long for him to be in an accident and smash the car. The car was fixable and I was able to drive the car home from the body shop. That was my first and last time driving it, because a year or two later he totaled the car completely.

After his dad passed away, he made fewer trips back to South Dakota with the exception of a few high school reunions. It was sometime in 2005 when he called me to visit about his health issues. He smoked and drank very hard as long as I can remember. Early in 2006, he called and said he was in the hospital and very sick. He said his lungs were bad and needed oxygen all the time. Realizing the gravity of the situation, I said he needed to make peace with his maker before he entered eternity. He readily acknowledged his bad life and how he never went to church. Being led by the Spirit of God, I asked him if he realized he was a sinner and where he would spend eternity. He wasn't sure where he'd spend eternity, so I told him of Jesus' death on the cross and that all his sins could be forgiven. All he needed to do was to believe that and ask Him to come into his life and heart, which he did. He then followed up with a Baptist minister in town who had been praying for them for 20 years and inviting them to church. A few days later he called crying with joy because he believed God had forgiven all his sins. A few days later we got a call that he had passed away. What a day that will be when we see each other in heaven, and also get to meet our stepbrother Michael Edward Davis.

Where was God?

In spite of Jerry's behavior and attitude towards this new family, I was able to stay out of the conflict. Being much younger and having to share a room with him helped our relationship in later years. God allowed me to keep the lines of communication open. Because of this he was open to me in his last days to accept Christ into his heart.

After his passing away I was able to thank the Baptist pastor who prayed for his family for 20 years. No fruit for 20 years, yet he remained faithful. What a testament to his faithfulness to God! Little things done or words spoken years earlier helped lead the way to Jerry's openness and willingness to search for God's truth in his last days.

Siblings and Spouses/Step Brother Jerry and Lucky

12

A Kindergarten Drop Out

For some unknown reason, I became a kindergarten dropout. My mother told me later in life that I just didn't like school and I didn't like my teacher, who was my Uncle Sam (mom's brother.) For some reason, she let me stay at home. There was no choice when it came to first grade, as I had to attend in spite of my dislike for it. My report card shows that I was an average student in class. My citizenship report was less than desirable. On a 1 to 4 scale, with lower numbers indicating your child has never attained this, I received a zero in courteous, zero in dependable, zero in response to the suggestion and a zero in clean habits of speech and action. Boy, my uncle sure had it in for me. Thankfully with 4th grade came a different story with a different teacher. I became a B average student in classes and was average in citizenship.

I was watching a TV show recently, and the host asked a guest who it was that lit a candle in their life. I reflected on that same question. I can now say that my fourth and fifth grade teacher was the first person to light my spiritual candle. Not only did I go to a B average in my classes, but my citizenship report also went to a B. Sometime during these two years of school, she offered a small Bible to anyone who would memorize John 3:16. Since I was good at memorizing, I soon got my first Bible and was so proud of it. I kept it for many years. One of the people that I will look up in heaven will be Ellen Kleinsasser, a real candle lighter.

The next three years under a new teacher worked pretty smooth. My grades were in the C+ to B- range with good citizenship. Of course there were a few exceptions in obeying school rules, being courteous, and not responding to suggestions. There must've been a lot of sickness those three years since I missed about 30 days a year... or perhaps mother didn't have the heart to be tough on me and force me to go to school.

After the first two years, I begin to enjoy school more and it showed in my behavior. Recess and lunch hour were fun times where we played kick the can a lot. My uncle put up two basketball hoops and helped clear the ground so that it was nice and smooth. The school district must have purchased new desks one year and they came in large boxes. All the boxes were saved in the horse barn on the school grounds. We had loads of fun making long tunnels with the boxes and even small rooms to crawl into. If memory serves me right, we hoped to get some of the girls to crawl in the tunnel. For some reason I have no memory of that ever happening. Many times in warm weather we would hike west to a small creek. We loved watching the turtles and even throwing rocks at them. Much of our time in nice weather was spent shooting hoops outside. In colder weather, we drew circles on the basement walls and pretended to shoot the basketball into the circles to score. With the ceiling so low there were no long shots. We also played London Bridges Falling Down inside when it was cold.

It was during my seventh and eighth grade years that my older brothers were involved in basketball and track at Yale High School. Their achievements inspired me enough that I did some preparation for our annual "Y Day", held in town. Several area schools were invited to a day of activities. Since my brother was a good broad jumper, I decided to do something like that myself. Somewhere I found a 2" x 12" x 3' board and dug a trench behind the boys' out house and place the board in that trench. Running from the schoolyard westward, I practiced jumping into the plowed fields to get ready for Y Day. In the spring of 1958, I won first place in the four events I entered. These events were high jump, shot put, broad jump and the 75 yard dash. I have saved those ribbons for all these years as a reminder of that achievement. How foolish it seems now to have kept them, but at the time, they gave me inward satisfaction.

One of our teachers got the bright idea of how we could have hot lunches in school. The Johnson school had two floor furnaces with grates over the top. Before long, we were having baked potatoes, hotdogs and other hot dishes by laying our food on the grates. The whole school smelled like baked potatoes from about 10:30 till noon. If you forgot to put your food on the furnace you were in trouble.

During my early years of school, I started out as a lefty. I don't remember if there was some social stigma about that, but I remember all the teachers were trying to get me to write right-handed on the chalkboard while helping me to learn cursive writing on the blackboard. While I was at my desk, I always felt like writing with my left hand. To this day, I ended up being right-handed in everything including writing on a blackboard except on paper where I still write left-handed. Perhaps you are as confused about that as I am.

Since we lived 2 1/2 miles from school, there were many occasions we had to walk both ways to school. At that time, it didn't seem like any big deal because other kids had to walk as well. If the weather was bad, someone managed to come and pick us up. For some reason, we all accepted this and managed in spite of bad weather to get to school.

One of the things we always looked forward to was the YCL meetings held in Huron. Although I don't remember what the meetings were all about, it sure was a good time to look around for cute girls. One of the girls I got to sit by agreed to a couple dates when we got to high school. A rather embarrassing thing happened at the start of our first date to the state fair grand stand. The 1949 Ford two-door car I drove was always getting changes to look cooler. It was hard to make this six-cylinder, straight stick, faded red Ford to look cool. I painted it black, put on full moon chrome hubcaps, and I installed blue lights around the interior. I made changes to the back of my seat so it reclined by having a bolt placed in the round hole behind the seat. Somehow, that bolt happened to slide in too far and my back rest fell completely against the back seat just as we were driving out of her yard. Much of the evening was spent trying to explain how something like that could've happened. In the end, we both had a good laugh over the incident.

Even though there was a certain amount of misbehaving on my part, I never got in a lot of serious trouble. One time when a big kid in the desk in front of me kept putting his head back and pushing my books down, I decided he needed a lesson in manners. I sharpened two pencils very sharp and held them up so when he pushed his head back to move my books, he met with my two pencils. Boy was he mad when I drew blood! My poor teacher did not know who to punish. We both got off free of any punishment.

Where was God?

In each of the chapters as I try to answer the question that is posed here, I can't help but go back and reflect on what did happen. Even though we may not realize it at the time, the Spirit of God was trying to touch us, to teach us, and to lead us closer to Him. Oh how refreshing it is to find these different people that I call candle lighters who helped me on my spiritual journey. Even though I was never able to relate my experience to my 4-5th grade teacher, I was able to tell her daughter what her mother had done for me and how she touched my life. May we all share our stories to encourage others to walk in the light of Christ!

(Johnson School Days)

(Proof of athletic achievement and proof of lack of academic achievement)

13

Life on the Farm

None of us were prepared for the shock we were in for once we arrived on the farm. I would call it a good day-bad day kind of feeling. Not being able to go where and when we wanted to was hard to take. For the most part we seem to settle in to a new house and a new life pretty well. It didn't take long before we realize this new life meant very hard work. Since I was the youngest I had the easiest job of gathering eggs, feeding chickens and ducks. The older boys were soon into milk cows and hauling manure. As I got older running the separator was my job as well as giving each of the cows some oats and hay during milking. Since all the calves were taken off the cows for milking there were lots of pale calves to be taken care of. Our old barn was designed quite well for all of this. Along the west side were about 10 stanchions to lock the cows in for milking. There was a gutter behind all the cows that needed cleaning after each milking. With all the cows and calves in the barn and the hayloft full of hay the barn was quite warm in winter but lots of flies in the summer. The two windows in the milking area served as a place for us to throw manure out the window. By the time spring came the pile was up to the bottom of the window. I liked having the two piles there because it served as a place for me to back our pony in between the piles and then someone would chase a calf out. I would then try to rope the calf. It was just all for fun and I never did get very good at it.

The chicken house had to be cleaned often as well. We just threw the manure out the window. Come spring it all had to be loaded on a manure spreader and hauled to the field. For some reason rats like to hide in the chicken manure pile and one year we had quite a time. Every time we stuck our pitchforks into the manure we came out with a rat or two. Our dog was going crazy as some went running across the yard. As I think back about those rats they were some of the biggest and fattest I have ever seen.

For many years mother had setting hens in the attic of the chicken house where she hatched eggs. There were about a dozen boxes where she put the hens in to sit on the eggs and another box to cover the hens to keep her on the nest. I would go with mother to feed and water the hens and then make sure they went back on the nest. The fun time came when the hatching began and we could move the little checks to another house and put them under this little tent heater. The chicks would walk under it and come out to eat at will.

Work was a big part of our life but we did have a social life. We often went to visit mom's family in Carpenter, Doland and Bridgewater. We also had great times when our parents visited with neighbors who had kids our own age. We had no TV to watch so we often played double canasta in the evenings and made homemade ice cream. For years we did not have a phone. Once we did get a phone we were on a party line. This meant that a number of your neighbors are on the same line and you could not use it if someone else was talking. There could be anywhere from 5 to 10 people on this line. Imagine our frustration when certain neighbors were talking for hours and tying up the line. You had to lift the plunger up and down to show people you needed to make a call. Imagine young lovers talking and you could actually listen to their love talk.

In the early days we did not have a bathroom in the house. The outhouse was outside and about 100 feet away. Toilet paper was not used but a Sears catalog served that purpose. In winter I strung an electric cord to the outhouse and put a small barn eater inside. We thought we really had it made them. Later on my step dad bought an indoor potty and installed it in the basement. It even had an exhaust pipe attached to the chimney. This potty was only 3 feet from the coal furnace. Even though we had to go downstairs through an old rock walled step to a dirt floor we had it made. So we now had an indoor warm toilet with soft toilet paper to use. Unfortunately my stepdad had to carry out the 20 gallon pail to be emptied every so often.

Later in life we were able to get a real indoor bathroom. We also were able to eliminate the Cobb burner in the kitchen and replace it with a propane heater in the floor. A steel grate covered the furnace. It was a great place to dry clothes and to get warm. Because this grate was very hot it presented itself as a great danger as well. I remember my young niece falling and getting branded for life on her stomach by the hot grate.

For bathing we use an oval portable galvanized tub. Water was heated on the stove and we all use the same water. Since I was the youngest I got to go first. Because the water was very hard you needed a lot of soap. The water got very cloudy in the first use. I was only five or six and didn't realize that passing gas in the tub was not a good idea. Unfortunately my brother Larry was the next in and reached for a bar of soap. What he thought was a bar soap did not make him happy when he went to wash himself. Of course mom had to pour out the water and start over again. Boy my siblings never let that happened again.

For many years we had no TV. I listened to our Motorola radio every night after school and Saturday morning. Some of the stories I listened to were: Bobby Benson and the B bar B riders, The Shadow knows, Sgt. Preston of the Yukon, The Lone Ranger, Gene Autry, The Cisco kid, Red Ryder, Sky King, Straight Arrow, Tarzan, and Tom mix. My first experience with TV was when my older brothers were invited to the home of the local grocery store owner. I remember watching it and this guy was talking while standing in a blizzard. The picture would fade in and out. It would be years later before we had our own TV.

Where was God?

Religion was not a big part of our lives growing up. It seems we were too busy with life to let any religion alter or effect out life style. We were all baptized as infants as required by our parents faith. Even though our father was gone mother expected us to continue in church tradition to get confirmed. Out of our deep respect for her all four of us were confirmed into the Lutheran church. Much later in life I was reminded by a member that part of my commitment to the church was to never leave. My response was yes I left that church but found Jesus Christ as my personal savior. Years later all three of us boys did leave the church to join other denominations. Had I taken the time to study Luther's doctrine of the just shall live by faith, perhaps church would've played a bigger part in my life. I'm sure that God's Spirit was speaking to me through these early years. A cold heart does not make for a good listener.

Acting Cool on the Farm

14

Learning the Meaning of Hard Work

From the time we moved to the farm until we left to go our separate ways, we knew about hard work. Moving to the farm proved to be the greatest learning experience of our lives. Had we stayed in town running the streets who knows what we might have become!

We spent our days doing many chores: chickens, ducks and geese had to be fed and we gathered eggs, cleaned them and stacked them in crates. We cleaned manure out of the chicken house and put fresh straw in the nests. We filled the kitchen cob box. We mixed oats in the barrel with milk and water to slop the hogs. We separated milk by cranking the separator, fed the milk cows oats and hay during milking, we fed pale calves with milk bottles, and helped feed cows in the pasture by pitching hay or cane over the fence. We picked rocks with stone boat pulled by horses. We dragged and disked fields, planted grain, windrowed and harvested. We mowed and put up alfalfa, cut cane and shocked, and stripped grass. We fixed fence and cultivated and harvested corn.

Learning to plow with a 3/16 bottom plow was a challenge as often times, that plow proved to be too much for our small Allis Chalmers tractor. Many times the plow would unhook when you hit a rock, which happened many times in one round. Later we were able to buy a trip beam plow that lifted when you hit a rock and then sprung back so there was no stopping. Then we even got a hydraulic lift on the plow. Not having a cab on the tractor made it miserable because dirt would blow up in your face as you plowed.

Along with the normal ground preparation, we learned to harvest as well. Our first combine was a 6 foot Case. Later we moved up to a G4 Minneapolis Moline. I ran this combine for several years with a MM pick up that jumped out of times often throughout the day. It was always fun trying to unplug the cylinder if too much grain entered the combine at one time!

Much of the intense labor involved cutting, stacking or baling hay. Stacking was done with the WG Allis Chalmers narrow front with a F10 farmhand loader. Once the large basket in front of the loader was filled with hay, a stack would be started (usually about 25 feet wide and 45 feet long.) The loader had long cylinders on each side that lifted the hay up so you would set it down on top of the pile. You moved around the stack as you lifted the hay higher and higher until the cylinder ended. As the hay got higher, you needed to drive up to the stack. There were several occasions that the loader began to tip and I had to release the cylinders and let the basket drop on the stack in order to keep the tractor from tipping over. Luckily I was never hurt. Mother would often comment on how nice I was able to stack hay, stating that it looked like it could be loaf of bread. In the earlier days, ditch hay had to be picked up by hand, loaded on a hayrack and pulled into the barn by slings and horses. A rope was pulled in the hay mound so the hay then dropped into the barn. On one occasion, a friend was helping and threw his pitchfork into the hayrack. The pitchfork stuck in my brother Larry's calf. Of course he needed a tetanus shot to make sure he was okay. One windy day while I was stacking hay in a field, a bunch of hay fell on the motor. I didn't notice it and did not take long for a fire to start. The ball under the gas tank often leaked and soon it was in flames. I looked for some dirt to throw the flames but even that did not stop it. I knew it would soon blow if I didn't get away. I started to run and heard the explosion behind me. I was not injured but the tractor was totaled. For some reason my step father loved the Allis Chalmers tractor. And AC was not my choice because I had driven a John Deere 4020's and I could steer it with one finger. Jones Company in Huron did not have a new AC so I suggested we go to the John Deere dealer and see Archie. We asked about a 4020 John Deere only to be shown the list of people who were waiting for a new one. It would be weeks or maybe months before we could get our order filled. After I explained we only needed to replace our loader tractor, he told us a semi just arrived from Canada with two 2510's on it. With the insurance money we purchased one of them and had the old F10 loader installed on the tractor. That tractor stayed with me until I quit farming in 1995. Later I had a Larson cab with the heater installed. It also had a kind of skylight so you could look up and see the loader as it was being raised to stack hay.

Another really difficult task was trying to shock cane that was 9 foot tall. The cane was cut and tied in bundles by a machine. We had to pick up two bundles, lean them together to stand and then start stacking more bundles around these two. Eventually this came to look like a tepee. You would continue to stack bundles until you had a nice shock that could withstand the wind. Later the shocks were hauled home on a hayrack, re-stacked and eventually fed to the cows.

One of the really frustrating experiences was in trying to cultivate corn. The John Deere cultivator was very heavy and was mounted to the WD on the front sides and the rear of the tractor. Since chemicals were not use like they are today, the row crops were filled with a weed called

Creeping Jenny. There were years when you only went a few feet and the cultivator would be plugged up. This really tested our patience. We were constantly stopping, backing up and getting off to unplug. Some years we had to cultivate the corn three or four times. The last time was always around the Fourth of July. Of course that meant no one was going to the lake.

In the early days, harvesting the corn was done by hand and very slow. My job was to drive the horses and the triple box while my brothers picked and threw the corn in the box. I remember always being cold and tired by the time we got home. Later on we used a pull type corn picker that made it a lot easier.

A never ending task on the farm was fencing. All holes for new posts were dug by hand. Most of the time you would dig a few inches fill the hole with water and then dig a little bit more the next day. Nothing was fast with fencing. We did not rebuild a lot of fences in my early years. My stepdad had a saying as he patched and patched some more. I used to get quite upset and angry as he would patch the fence and say "Oh hell, it'll do for now." The older I got, the more I started fences from scratch because fences needed to look neat. I guess that's why now I'm kind of fussy about neatness and looks.

Even though we were always busy working at home, we found it necessary to work outside of the home in order to make some money. During my high school years, I worked for several farmers. Since I was driving the tractor and a very early age, my parents gave me a lot of freedom. When I was about 10 or 11 years old, I was asked to take our Allis Chalmers tractor and pick up a trailer of oats about a mile from the farm. My friend from town was visiting at the time. Off we went, wide open south of the yard, turned west by the pasture and then turned south before we hit the cornfield. Slowing down to make a turn didn't enter my mind since we were having a good time. Because the tractor had a narrow front and it started to slide a bit so I hit the left break to make it head south. Unfortunately I applied a little too much break and the tractor began to spin around heading the exact direction we just came from. Before I knew what was happening, I felt like something was pushing me face down on the rear end of the tractor. This should not have been possible because my friend was sitting on the toolbox on the fender. When reality set in, I was looking up at the sky snugly located between the seat and the fender without a scratch. What had just happened and I how did I get in this location? Crawling out from under the tractor, I looked up and saw my friend walking out of the cornfield. With the wheels still spinning on the upside down tractor, we both stood dumbfounded for some time. My friend was thrown about 30 feet into the cornfield but came walking out without a scratch.

Needing spending money, I went to work for a neighbor who was a Holdeman (also known as a member of the Church of God in Christ Mennonite) for five dollars a day. I mostly plowed from sunrise to sunset with a four bottom plow that would not go into the ground. The points of the lays were completely worn down. I eventually ended up plowing furrows across the end to help it go into the ground. At the end of a long day, which was not about to end, I was told we have to head to Manchester to pick up a load of bales. The truck had a bale loader mounted to the driver's side of the truck. Darkness soon fell upon us, but the boss told me to keep driving. With very poor visibility, a very sleepy and inexperienced driver, I was driving over more bales than I was picking up. Somehow we got the truck full and headed home. Eating supper at 10:30 was not something I was used to. I assumed that since we worked so late, my morning hours the next day would change. No such luck! My orders were to report at 7 AM the next day. I lasted there about two weeks and then quit. They did have great food and the best tea I ever had.

My experience in running our IH tractor with a G4 combine got me a lot of harvesting jobs. I was able to secure a job with my uncle and his brother during the summer. They ran two G4 combines that had melrow pickups. I was lucky because they picked up grain five times better and did not jump out of time. Since I had never worked by the hour, I thought my time started when we got outside and ended when we walked into the house at night. Little did I realize that being paid a dollar an hour meant machine time hours. This means you only get paid when the combine is running. The first time I turned in my hours, I was questioned if that was machine time hours. I felt like crawling in a hole, but my aunt came to my rescue and said they shouldn't have expected me to know what hours to write down. After some recalculation on my part, I was paid my wages. With the check I bought my boss's 1949 Ford six-cylinder straight stick car.

For several years I found a unique source of income for myself by stripping grass. We rented 100 acres of grass that I was able to strip the seeds off and sell. Many ditches also had June grass that provided seed. The seeds were sacked up and later sold in town at the seed store. These machines had 2' cylinders with spikes sticking out and spun, causing seeds to fly back into the box. I could make between $100 and $200 by selling grass seed. This pay was good, but it was hot, sticky work and there were lots of bees to watch out for. Grass fields usually had lots of badger holes big enough that a narrow front end of a tractor could fall into them. Sometimes the tractor would hit one and come to a sudden stop and almost throw you off the seat. I tried several things to keep this from happening, including placing a 2 x 4 board between the front wheels to keep the front end from falling too deep. I was lucky as I never broke a front end off of the tractor.

Every year a neighbor and his partner hired men to go south to combine. My cousin had already agreed to go and said they were looking for one more man. The job required someone to have grain hauling experience. I was only 15 and had never been away from home and was somewhat inexperienced at truck driving, but they hired me anyway. I agreed to work for an hourly wage but when the bosses decided to keep track of my hours, I had a very serious problem. My excitement of going had overshadowed the details of room costs, food costs, etc. We headed south to Hardtner, Kansas (a few miles from Oklahoma) where we had work lined up. After several days of combining it started to rain. We were shut down for 10 days in this little town. With no work, we shot a lot of pool and drank a few Coors beers. One of the crewmembers was a wino who called everybody "Booger". Most of his time was spent drinking cheap wine. Every night my cousin and I would go behind the hotel and find several partially filled bottles of wine lying around. He would drink some, go hide it, forget where he put it, and then go buy some more. Finally, our boss was able to get a big job west of town combining oats. Since we did not bring any pickup heads, they went to a nearby town and purchased two. When that was completed, that farmer had us do his wheat. One of his fields had recently had a new approach installed and as I was pulling out of the field and turning onto the road, the fresh dirt gave way and the truck full of wheat slid into the ditch. It was too full and risky to pull out full so we needed to unload some of the wheat. Finally with one combine pulling forward and one combine pulling from the side to keep it from tipping over we got it on the road. After this happened, there were a few choice words directed my way. Being right in my face, I couldn't help but smell whiskey and lemon on his breath. Refreshments were always on the front seat of their vehicles. I guess the help drove them to drinking!

Moving was always the hardest part of the work. Tearing the sides off the truck and moving the 3" x 12" railroad planks along the floor as the combine was being driven onto the truck. My cousin and I were glad we never had to drive the truck with the combine on the back.

With the head on, it stuck out quite a bit on both sides. Our wino friend was a little hung over as we headed north through Kansas and Nebraska. While on a high overpass, we met traffic that caused them to pull over to the right. He forgot that the header could hit a light pole that reached well above the highway. Sure enough the outside header caught the light pole causing major damage to the head. My cousin was asked to drive the truck until we arrived at our next destination and my boss sent the wino home on a bus. After six weeks on the road, we arrived home. The next day we headed to church and parked north of the church. My boss came out of this house and handed me a check. Not knowing what was spent for motel rooms, food costs and lost time from rain, I had no idea what to expect. After looking at the check, my heart sank because I was sure I was worth more than $138 for 6 weeks of work. Like my mother used to say, you live and learn.

Where was God?

Little did I realize that all of these work-related experiences would be utilized later in life in so many ways. Through all of my hard work experiences, I learned the value of self-worth and the building of character. It is now easy to see God's purpose, His help and His protection through these many jobs. I learned many skills by performing these jobs that I've used through my life. Growing up I was called on many times to utilize these skills in fixing things for my mother. Later in life, my nephews would call my brother and me "the MacGyver brothers," which was after a TV show from the 1980s about a guy that could improvise or fix things in a very inventive way by using whatever is at hand.

15

Pressure to Perform

Growing up under the shadow of two older brothers and one stepbrother, I felt others held certain expectations of me. People make certain assumptions about you that are often based on your older brothers' accomplishments. Even though I was somewhat successful in track in grade school, that didn't register with me that I could be good in high school. Coaches have a way of assuming that you will perform as well as, or maybe better than, your brothers. There were many occasions I was asked if I would be as fast as my brother. Some even hinted that maybe I could win the state track meet all alone. Having a brother earn four firsts in the 1957 state track meet did not help. Such a feat would require more commitment and dedication that I cared to put forth. So with some natural ability, little desire, no goals and many other interests, I stumbled through my school days with minor success.

Never in all my school years did I ever have a coach sit down with me to talk about establishing goals in light of my abilities. Not only that, but I was never taught anything about techniques, time expectations, or ways to improve. Our workouts consisted of being timed in the hundred yard dash on the first day of practice, and running four and a half miles south to highway 14 and back.

I will never forget my first track meet. We headed to Redfield for their annual invitational. Before the meet the coach told us what events we were expected to participate in. When he came to my name and read off the events he put me in, I could've crawled in a hole. I was going to run the high hurdles as a freshman, never having practiced at all! I was told that my brothers were both great hurdlers, and I didn't have the fortitude to say no, so I ran the hurdles. After falling down four times, I managed to finish but I was badly skinned up. I never ran the hurdles again after that day. That same coach asked me to find my own ride to Sioux Falls for the state track meet. Since the coach didn't think it was important enough for him to be there, my attitude wasn't too good. Needless to say, because of my poor attitude I didn't do well and did not place.

Not meeting the expectations of coaches and others was not helpful in other challenges in life. What happens when we continue to fall short of others' expectations of us, rather than being satisfied with our own expectations? When entering college, I experienced the same attitude. I was always being forced to live in the shadows of others and their performances. Most of my energy was spent trying to figure out where I came in on this game called life. It seems funny now as I look back and wonder why I never felt those expectations in the academic arena. Whatever the expectations of others might have been, I never let that interfere with the directions I was handed. Without a doubt, life would have been much easier had I taken advantage of all the opportunities throughout my educational experience. There are many things that I would like to have a second chance at but life only goes around one time and we need to make the best choices for today and not live in the past.

Where was God?

I believe that God granted me just enough success in sports to carry me through many tough times. Encouragement from others was enough to keep me going. If we all tried to live life according to other people's expectations, we would never find out who God wants us to be. There is nothing better than the peace and contentment we can now get from following God's roadmap. We can always do this by walking through the doors He opens for us after a lot of prayer. I have realized many times that pushing open the closed door may lead to trouble behind that door.

Hoop Time at Johnson School

16

Troubled Teens

A. Life Without Boundaries

Most kids my age would've loved to live a life without boundaries. My stepfather never interfered in mother's child rearing practices, whatever they were. I don't know if my older siblings had the same latitude that I had. Maybe she just wore herself out on them and gave up on me. For whatever reason I pretty much did as I pleased. I could leave when I wanted to and come home when I wanted to. If I were to guess as to how mother got that way it would seem that she just didn't have the inner strength to put up a fight. I have no memory of her ever giving any of us a spanking…with one exception. She took a belt to one of my older brothers. It must not have hurt too much because he turned around and laughed at her and said his billfold and handkerchief kept him from getting hurt. Mother was more concerned with her stepson because he never listened to her and was often mean. One such occasion was when she reminded him that he hated marshmallows with toasted coconuts after he had eaten half a bag. After realizing what he had eaten, he declared he hated them and threw the remaining bag at mother as he stomped away.

At a very early age, I started going with two or three older guys to movies and roller-skating. During many of these outings we indulged in drinking wine with 7-Up, peppermint schnapps or beer. I'm sure that there were times that consumption was in excess. Even though we were all under age, there was always someone who would purchase beverages for us. None of us were ever stopped or got into trouble because of it. I can say for myself that someone was always looking out for me.

Ever since high school, I had some kind of car. After working for my uncle one summer, I purchased his 1949 Ford. It didn't look like much as it was a faded red, but it ran. In those days it was cool to put lowering blocks in the backend. There wasn't much else I could do to the car but I did later have it painted black. It's funny how wheels of any kind can give one a certain amount of freedom. Having wheels and access to my parents' gas tank was all that I needed.

One rainy night in town, I let a girlfriend drive this '49 Ford. As she turned the corner on Third Street heading north on Dakota Avenue, she was having trouble seeing because of the rain. My window wipers quit working and I was moving a rod back and forth underneath the dash to make the wipers work to try and clear the window. She got too close to a parked car, bending my fender back until it was hitting the tire. We pried the fender back and decided to go have breakfast and think things through. The girls were taken home before we headed west on Market Road to a restaurant. There was an old train car on the north side of the street that served food all night. After breakfast, we headed back to the scene and called the cops. My story was my wipers broke and I reached down to clear the window and we hit the other car. The cops bought the story and so did my folks. I eventually arrived home around 4 AM. Later in high school, I traded up to a 1956 Ford Fairlane two-door sedan. This car was a V-8 with a straight stick shift. To make it cool I put in a floor shift, added continental fender skirts, put on dual headers with glass pack mufflers and straight pipe headers under each door. These caps could be taken off to make the car very loud. Taking off the caps and driving down Main Street late at night or early morning seemed like a good idea. The noise it made sounded like a dozen Harleys.

Seldom did I stay home on Saturday or Sunday nights. On many occasions we went to Huron to a movie, went roller-skating or just cruising. Often we went to DeSmet to pick up girls, drove to Huron, went to a drive in, back to DeSmet to take the girls home and then home. Often times in boredom we thought of foolish things to do. One of these was letting a little air out of the tires and driving to Huron on the road tracks. The tires just fit on the rails and we drive about 40 miles an hour with no hands. What about trains coming from either direction? We never gave it any thought. I also raced from Yale to Highway 14 with a friend who had a 56 Chevy. We were side-by-side traveling about 105 miles an hour. Not wanting to give up as we approached Highway 14, I was unable to stop and went across the highway into the ditch sliding sideways in the ditch heading west. I passed several cars that stopped for us and then went back on the highway headed to town. Later I learned from Tubby the County Sheriff that he was one of the cars watching us as we traveled across the highways. He told us to cool it a little bit in the future because he knew who we were.

One time some girls invited us to a birthday party south of Doland. Because this was the night before a big basketball game, we decided to leave early. Getting to my car we realized that the girls had let air out of our tires so we could not leave. By the time we got air and returned home it was after midnight. The next day our coach found out about this and was not very happy. I think somebody squealed on us. I was very tired after getting home from school so I took a three hour nap. That night I played one of my better games as we played Iroquois, a big rival. After the game my coach commented that maybe we should stay out late more often because of the way we played.

Basketball players were expected to drive ourselves to all away games. One night one of my passengers pulled out a half pint of schnapps on the way to Bonilla. After being double dared, we all took a couple of slugs. As we huddled before the game our coach looked at us in a strange way. Noticing that he realized something was strange, we said we just brushed our teeth with some peppermint toothpaste. After the game he complimented us in that he had never seen us play so loose. This was another win for our team but another nightmare for our parents.

Where was God?

It now is a mystery to me how I could have lived the life I lived without getting in trouble. The fact that we never did get in trouble with the law because of drinking and driving is a testament to the fact that someone was surely watching out for us. Even though I was not living life as a Christian, it was God's grace and mercy that watched over me through very troubling times. I cannot fathom how God can love someone even though that person continues to live a godless life. Romans 5:8 reminds us "but God commended his love towards us, in that, while we were yet sinners, Christ died for us."

Yale Basketball team

B. A PHILOSOPHY TO LIVE BY

During my youth I never realized that I had a philosophy that I was living by. Looking back at things said, along with written comments and actions taken, I now realize otherwise. Even though I've never written them out, they were nevertheless lived out. I can now say much of my life at that time was governed by the following:

1. When wine, women and song get me down, I'll quit singing.

2. I want to live fast, love hard, die young and leave a beautiful memory. (This was my senior year quote in the annual.)

3. Live life with reckless abandonment.

I now wonder what the reason was for such a fatalistic approach to life. I now share my story of the first 20 years of life as lost, lonely and loveless. Feeling lost as I ran the streets alone for the first five years. With mother working at the restaurant and doing ironing for people, she didn't have time to pay attention to all four of us. Throughout all those growing up years I never heard from anyone the three little words that we all long for. No one said "I love you." What does one learn from old guys in the pool hall drinking, cussing and playing cards? The only thing that was uplifting to me was when the postmaster called me "Scooter" or "Superman." I liked those names.

Moving to the farm did not change any of those feelings. My family and I never developed any emotional bonds with our new stepdad. I never knew how a normal family should interact. I can say no physical contact or emotional expressions of love were ever received. My mother was never a hugging and kissing type of person but we all know the life altering sacrifices she made for us. She made decisions that were always in the best interest of her kids and that may have included this marriage. I was lonely for some kind of relationship with anyone that really cared about me. I was feeling loveless because I never experienced that feeling. The reality of what was going on inside was undetected by my high school classmates. If asked, I'm sure most would think I had the world by the tail. I was never a studious person but fairly popular and an average athlete. In my high school days it was a normal thing to take a class popularity poll (see the following polls from my junior years and senior years). You can see that I was not the most dignified, most likely to succeed, most dependable, most cheerful, best student, most studious, best sport, or most talkative. Being popular in these polls never translated into self-worth for me. It seems our soul longs for something deeper and more meaningful. Thank God I later found it.

The façade I wore that all is well seemed reasonable in my high school days. It was a lot easier to wear the mask of everything is great rather than letting reality show through. One of the greatest struggles in life occurred during my junior year at school. I was so tormented with life that I told my mother that I didn't want to live anymore. Her advice was a standard cliché, "you are young and you have your whole life ahead of you." I thought to myself, "Sure mom, you mean my whole miserable life."

Most of my youth was spent living like I was in a hurry to get somewhere. Never did I think of where the road I was on would lead to. I possess a profound and deep sadness as to why someone didn't pick up on these feelings of unhappiness. Not having grandparents, uncles or older brothers around during my high school days added to this lack of direction. Everyone needs a go-to person in their deepest hour of need. Never did I feel that there was anyone that I could confide in.

It didn't help that during my early years on the farm, a local gas delivery person asked me if I would ever amount to a damn. That question haunted me for years. Why would he say that every time he came? What does he see in me that would cause him to say that? Years later I saw this person sweeping the arena floor. May the Lord forgive me for going alongside him as he swept the floor and asking him if he'll ever amount to a damn. Negative words spoken to a young child are not soon forgotten.

This somewhat fatalistic philosophy materialized out of a lack of an affirmation of my uniqueness as a person, verbal expressions of being needed and lack of physical contact. Maybe that's why later in life I realized I was looking for love in the wrong places.

Where was God?

Anyone who has lived 20 years in darkness while feeling lost, lonely and loveless hopes for a better life. I believe that God puts candle lighters in our paths to lead us to God. This may come in the form of kind words, good deeds or words from Scripture. Now as I look back, in spite of this fatalistic attitude, there were times when God's people would try to shine a little light in my life.

We are all born with an inward longing for something greater than ourselves. It's funny that we often look for this something in the world we live in. John 14:6 tells us that Jesus says "I am the way, the truth and the life." Only there can we find fullness of life. Much of my time and talents were wasted during this time of my life. My only redemption is that hopefully now all of God's gifts are being utilized for his kingdom and glory. Having lived in the darkness for so long makes me more excited to now live in the light of His love and shine that love in the dark corners of others who live in darkness.

Popularity Poll of 1959-1960

Girls		Boys
Shirley Tschetter	Most Popular	Ronnie Weidner
Shirley Tschetter	Best Looking	Ronnie Weidner
Inge Kautz	Most Dignified	Benny Boetel
Jeanine Maass	Prettiest Hair	Ronnie Weidner
Deanna Ulrich	Prettiest Teeth	Ron W. Phil G
Margo Boetel	Biggest Flirt	Ronnie Weidner
Deanna Ulrich	Whittiest	Phil Glanzer
Rilla Bogh	Most Bashful	Benny Boetel
Inge Kautz	Likely to succeed	Phil Glanzer
Shirley Tschetter	Dependable	Phil Glanzer
Shirley Tschetter	Best figure	Bill Hofer
Margo B Deanna B	Best dancer	Ronnie Weidner
Jeanine Maass	Most cheerful	Tony Gross
Margo Boetel	Best Athlete	Ronnie Weidner
Kathleen Hofer	Best Musician	Bruce Beckman
Inge Knutz	Best student	Phil Glanzer
Deanne Boetel	Puppy lovers	Delano Gross
Inge Keutz	Most studious	Benny Boetel
Jeanine Maass	Best sport	Bill Hofer
Jeanine Maass	Prettiest eyes	Phil Glanzer
Patsy Glanzer	Neatest	Ronnie Weidner
Jeanine Maass	Prettiest lips	Ronnie Weidner
Margo B Deanna U	Best complexion	Keith Glanzer
Sheila Hofer	Silliest	Paul Farrell
Merolyn Boetel	Biggest blusher	Benny Boetel
Deanna Ulrich	Most artistic	Robert Ulrich
Shirley Tschetter	Best peronality	Delano Gross
Sheila Hofer	Most talkative	Tillman Hofer
Patty Glanzer	Best dressed	Ronnie Weidner

Margo Boetel	Hitched	Tony Gross
Inge Kautz	**Biggest vocabulary**	Phil Glanzer
Deanna Boetel	**Peppiest**	Paul F. Keith G
Jeanine Maass	**Most versatile**	Ronnie Weidner
Inge Kautz	**Biggest asset to school**	Dale Hofer
Inge Kautz Mergo Boetel	**Applepolishers**	Dale Hofer
Sheila Hofer	**Biggest tease**	Tony Gross
Margo Boetel	**Prettiest legs**	Bill Hofer

Popularity Poll
of 1960-1961

Girls		Boys
Patty Glanzer	Most Popular	Ronnie Weidner
Paulette Hofer	Best Looking	Ronnie W. Bill Hofer
Janice Walter	Most Dignified	Phil Glanzer
Rita Ford	Prettiest Hair	Bill Hofer
Merolyn Boetel	Prettiest Teeth	Ronnie Weidner
Paulette Hofer	Biggest Flirt	Tony Gross
Kathy Ford	Whittiest	Paul Farrell
Janice Walter	Most Bashful	Raymond Boetel
Janice Walter	Likely to succeed	Phil Glanzer
Patty Glanzer	Dependable	Phil Glanzer
Paulette Hofer	Best figure	Ronnie Weidner
Rita Ford	Best dancer	Ronnie Weidner
Merolyn Boetel	Most cheerful	Douglas Tyrrell
Merolyn Boetel	Best Athlete	Ronnie Weidner
Kathleen Hofer	Best Musician	Gary Maas
Janice Walter	Best student	Phil Glanzer
Kathleen Hofer	Puppy lovers	Benny Boetel
Janice Walter	Most studious	Gary Maas
Merolyn Boetel	Best sport	Bill Hofer
Patty Glanzer	Prettiest eyes	Tony Gross
Patty Glanzer	Neatest	Ronnie Weidner
Paulette Hofer	Prettiest lips	Ronnie Weidner
Marlette Hofer	Best complexion	Keith Glanzer
Rita Ford	Silliest	Paul Farrell
Merolyn Boetel	Biggest blusher	Benny Boetel
Mary Eisenbeis	Most artistic	Gary Maas
Merolyn Boetel	Best peronality	Tony Gross
Rita Ford	Most talkative	Paul Ferrell
Patty Glanzer	Best dressed	Ronnie Weidner

Kathy Ford	**Hitched**	Ronnie Weidner
Patty Glanzer	**Biggest vocabulary**	Phil Glanzer
Merolyn Boetel	**Peppiest**	Paul Farrell
Patty Glanzer	**Most versatile**	Ronnie Weidner
Patty Glanzer	**Biggest asset to school**	Phil Glanzer
Mary Eisenbeis	**Applepolishers**	Terry Andersen
Kathy Ford	**Biggest tease**	Terry Andersen
Paulette Hofer	**Prettiest legs**	Ronnie Weidner

17

A Blond Joke

I must confess over the years I have told a few blonde jokes. Never in my wildest dreams could I imagine being on the receiving end of one of these jokes.

It was in my junior/ senior year in high school that I was living a boundary less, troubled youth with a strange carefree philosophy of life. I often managed to survey the horizon for good-looking girls. Sitting in the back of study hall, I could easily look across the room to check out the freshman girls. My sharp, cunning eye hit pay dirt when this blonde crossed my radar. I soon found out she was quiet, bashful and a "goodie two shoes" girl. The urban dictionary defines goodie two shoes as "a person, usually female, who tries to be as good and clean as humanly possible. She is more often than not a staunch conservative and takes pride in her virginity and her practice of abstinence. She is definitely a God-fearing girl who always goes to church every Sunday, and indeed, based on the way she dresses, she looks like she's going to church every day. She cannot abide it when people cuss in front of her-the most extreme goodie two shoes faint when hearing foul language-and of course she would never consider smoking, drinking, doing drugs, or having any physical contact with a boy beyond holding hands or perhaps a kiss on the cheek. Can be nice, but eventually begins to lecture you about your sinful lifestyle and just becomes a pest."

Having lived in the fast lane for so many years, I was sure that disqualified me from ever earning her affection. Being directionless and carefree, I thought, "What do I have to lose?" Guys have this built-in idea of how we began to put the moves on a girl. We began slowly by talking, kidding and joking and looking for vibes from a girl that would signal she likes me. Once this happens, you for sure can talk about dating. With her first no, I wondered how Puritanical her parents must be. After several no's and giving the excuse that she was too young, I thought about giving up. Anyone who really knows me would say he never gives up. One of my many faults is being stubborn.

Driving down Main Street after school one day, I saw this pretty blonde coming out of the grocery store with a bag of groceries. My instinct told me that this damsel in distress needed a ride home. She had this heavy loaf of bread and lived two whole blocks away. To my surprise, she accepted a ride home. Nearing her house, I saw a mother bear waiting in the driveway. As I pulled up beside her, I rolled down my window and waited for my lecture which I knew was coming. As I expected, she told me she's too young for me and she pointed to the road off their yard and gave me instructions to never return. I think if she would have told me I was not good enough for her daughter, I could've agreed with her. I pondered if my late-night or sometimes early morning drives through town with both headers wide-open had anything to do with her feelings about me.

Being persistent pests, we never gave up trying to get together. One day I was shocked to my core when she finally said yes to one of my requests to spend time together. Of course there was a slight catch to the date. We had to go to a Sunday night service at her church. I thought I knew what I was getting into and had things covered. Little did I realize the trap I was walking into. Never underestimate the power of a praying mother.

Growing up as I did attending a Catholic and a Lutheran Church, I had a concept of what a church service should be like. Since this was a Sunday night service, I wasn't sure what to expect because I had never been to church at night. Every preconceived notion I had about church was transformed that first visit. The service was very non-structured, laid-back, casual and very enjoyable. Several members got up and sang. Some gave readings and one of the members even got up and gave a little talk. I couldn't get over how members could actually get up behind the pulpit since I thought that was sacred ground. After the service, we were immediately invited to someone's house for ice cream and coffee. That sounded a little weird to me since I had never put the two together.

Looking back at that first meeting and trying to analyze what happened that night is almost indescribable. The joy and love that I saw in others' lives resonated in me. This was love that I had never felt before. Dr. David Jeremiah's book, 'The Signs of Life,' describes what a spirit filled church should look like. He gives five signs a church should have: 1. Dusty shoes, 2. Worn out knees, 3. Rolled up sleeves, 4. An open hand, and 5. Out-stretched arms. This sums up my feelings about this church, as over time I experienced all those from the body of Christ. Here I was thinking I would just do this church thing to get a date with a gal. Little did I realize that this blonde had caused the joke to be on me, because I didn't see the trap coming. I now call it the love trap. Looking back, I'm glad I got caught and since then have been forever set free.

Where was God

Even though my future mother-in-law once sent me down the road, she eventually ended up being my prayer warrior. The power of God to move someone from bitterness to love is hard to believe. She never told me of all her prayers for me, but I felt God's power pulling me towards Him. Looking back I can now say another piece of the puzzle of my life is in place and I understand. Another candle lighter showed up and did her part. I thank God for Grandma Dot and many others who prayed and loved me into God's kingdom.

Paulette and her mother/Paulette as a bridesmaid/ school picture/ grade school cheerleaders

18

I Saw the "Light"

How many of us have walked into a dark room and stumbled around lost and confused while looking for the light switch? We try our best to navigate our way through the darkness. Would you and I be able to describe the darkness to someone if they had never experienced it? Darkness is often characterized by the absence of something. How many of us go through life living in darkness? This is how I lived a good portion of my life. Analyzing my philosophy of life leads me to no other conclusion than I was living in total darkness. How is it that a person lives in total darkness and doesn't know? No, I was not blind physically, but I speak of spiritual blindness. This blindness was such that I had no reason for living. I never realized that I was longing for something inside that only the light of His truth could satisfy. We learned early in life that physical darkness is overcome by the presence of light. How do we get to the place in life to begin asking ourselves if we are really happy and content living in darkness? Our lack of understanding is what keeps us in our spiritual darkness. How do we get the light? Psalm 119:130 says the entrance or the unfolding of Your Word gives light.

After attending several church services, something became very real to me. These "church people," as I called them, were living a different lifestyle than what I knew. It was like they knew something really important about life that I did not understand. They had an inner glow that manifested itself in the way they treated me. I now realize they were not the source of the light but showed me the source of their inner glow. I have described these people as the ones who were responsible for loving me into the kingdom. They lit up my dark pathway by shining their light on the pathway that led to the true light, which is Christ Himself. Early on, I welcomed their confirmation of me as a worthy person. John 6:44 reminds us "No one can come to me unless the Father who sent me draws them." When our life is examined under the microscope of His Word, we soon find we are a sinful fallen people. Months later during a church service, the simplicity of all this was explained to me. The pastor said it was as simple as A B C. First comes the "C", which is "confession" of all our sins and fallen nature. With that we understand the penalty of our shortcomings. Next is "B", which stands for "believe" that Jesus paid it all. If life were a monopoly game, we would have a get out of jail free card. But in real life we escape not jail, but eternity in hell. We have this freedom only when we follow through and do "A", which is "accept" Jesus into our hearts to live and reign. The preacher at this little Mennonite country church, known better as the "big church in the community" was someone always on fire for the Lord with a spring in his step. It was during one of his alter calls that I felt the Lord calling me, so I went forward to accept Christ into my life. Later I was again baptized in the James River.

After living one fourth of my life outside the family of true believers, a great burden was lifted. Along with forgiveness of sins came the security of eternal life and comfort of being in His presence, no matter what trials may come. How could God love me so much that he would send his son to die for me, so that I could be held sinless?

Where was God?

Looking back on my life, I now see examples of light flashes when God was trying to get my attention. He used a teacher who taught me my first Bible verse. He used the tractor accident to get me thinking about death. He used sickness and surgeries to help me to realize there are some things in life we need help with. Life now makes more sense as our eyes are opened and our hearts are warmed by the rays of His love. The omnipresence of our God comforts us in that He was there every step we took in life. I have learned that when our hearts are open and soft to receive His light, we are then instructed to walk in the light. First John 1:5-7 says, "This is the message we have heard from him and declare to you: God is light; in him there is no darkness at all. If we claim to have fellowship with him and yet walk in the darkness, we lie and do not live out the truth. But if we walk in the light, as he is in the light, we have fellowship with one another, and the blood of Jesus, his Son, purifies us from all sin."

Anyone who has come to a point in life when the weight of sin is so heavy they cannot bear it any longer knows the feeling. When guilt hits you with all its power, we find ourselves with no excuse. That is "When mercy walked in", as sung by Gordon Mote and written by Stuart Keene Hine:

I stood in the court room the Judge turned my way
It looks like you're guilty now what do you say
I spoke up your honor I have no defense
But that's when mercy walked in

Mercy walked in and pleaded my case
Called to the stand God's saving grace
The blood was presented that covered my sin

Forgiven when mercy walked in

Praise the lord
I stood there and wondered how could this be
That someone so guilty had just been set free
My chains were broken I felt born again
The moment that mercy walked in

The blood was presented that covered my sin
Forgiven when mercy walked in

19

Graduated From High School, Now What?

There was very little thought or exploring that went into planning for my future. All my life up to this point was spent living in the moment. I always felt that the future would take care of itself. My world was very small and we were seldom confronted with different occupations. The extent of my career choice was limited by my mother, who said we should all be teachers. She said they get paid for twelve months, but only work nine months. (I don't think she was really aware of a teacher's salary at that time.)

As a senior, I did attend a career day at Huron College. To me, a Highway Patrol job looked exciting. Attending the workshop, I was told by the presenter of some of the more gruesome responsibilities of a law enforcement officer. I soon lost my desire to become a Highway Patrol officer.

In the late summer of 1961, while dragging a field just east of our farm, I was stopped by a gentleman. His name was Gary Wiren from Huron College, and he was the head track coach. Gary had seen me run track during my junior and senior year of high school and noted I did very well. I guess he was referring to the four firsts I got as a junior and three firsts and one second as a senior, at the Beadle County track meet. He was also well acquainted with my older brothers and their track accomplishments. All he had to do was wave a $100 track scholarship in my face, and I was headed to Huron College.

Luckily, I had taken the ACT, which was required for admissions. Since studying was not my strength, my score was not very respectable. Getting in 19 on the test actually looked pretty good to me, and it wasn't a problem getting into college.

I never gave a second thought to how I was going to pay for this education or what I would major in. I didn't know if my grades would be good enough, since in high school I pulled mostly a C average. But I threw caution to the wind since I had nothing to lose and I had nothing else going on.

Where was God?

In spite of our lack of planning, it seems God is often planning for us. Had the track coach not stopped that day, I'm not sure where my path in life would have taken me. Jeremiah 29:11 says. "for I know the plans I have for you, says the Lord, plans for your welfare, and not for calamity, to give you hope and a future." Mr. Wiren was used by God to help me make a decision to get into college.

Senior picture

Senior skip day

20

A Whole New World

This farm boy arrived on campus with a lot of insecurity. Going from a school with only 33 students to a campus of 450 was very frightening. Most of the kids seemed to be so much further ahead in social skills and career planning than I was. While visiting with a fellow freshman, I learned of his interest in becoming an architect. Remembering my joy in drawing pictures of barns, tractors and cars, I decided to major in architecture, without knowing anything about that field! Since math was my best ACT score, I was assigned a math teacher for my advisor. My advisor struggled a bit with my schedule for a pre-architectural program. My class load was a challenge, given I had taken only algebra one and geometry in high school, but no chemistry. This load was made more unbearable with my poor study habits. After getting my grades at the end of the first semester, I remember calling mom and telling her to come and get me because I was flunking out. She had asked what I was taking and my grades in each. I explained the classes and my grades that were 3 D's, 2 C's and 1 B. She encouraged me to stay in school, take easier classes and maybe change majors. Taking her advice, I ended the second semester with 2 C's and 5 B's, with most of those coming from PE classes. I was great in tumbling and stunts, but not so good in slide rule and first aid for some reason. In my chemistry class of 30 students, I was the dumbest one in the class. But in lab, I had some of the prettiest drawings of our work with beakers and tubes and so forth. I had no idea what my partner was doing with all the chemicals, but my diagrams were the envy of the whole class. My instructor would look at my notebook filled with drawings and smile. It got me a D in his class. I had a chance for an A, but blew my chance because of fear of failure. Dr. Strong placed a beaker full of oil of some kind on the desk at the beginning of the semester and noted how full it was. At the end of the class, he showed us that oil measurement and it was different. He offered an A to any student who could explain what caused this change. Even the smartest kids in class had no answer for him. I knew the answer, but my fear of being wrong in front of the whole class petrified me, so I froze. When he gave us the answer of specific gravity, I could have died. The A was mine to get, but fear of failure ruled my speech. I left class that day with the new inner pride and promised myself I would always speak up, no matter how dumb it might sound.

During my first year, I don't think I earned the hundred dollar track scholarship because my stepdad needed me for work in the spring. I did work out and attended a meeting or two, and even got a medal.

My second year went a lot better than the first. Since the tuition needed to be paid, I had to go to work and my grades continued to suffer. I just didn't know how to study. I ended up that second year first semester with 5 C's and 1 B. For the second semester I earned 2 A's, 2 B's and 3 D's. Oh, how I disliked my classes of History of the Hebrews and the life of Christ! Isn't it interesting how a person's attitude makes all the difference? Over the past 50 years I have devoted much of my time studying the Bible, which these two courses covered. My hunger for knowledge in His Word doesn't ever diminish.

My work schedule consisted of delivering clothes for the Huron Cleaners from 1 to 5 every day. After work, I grabbed a Coke and two new way sandwiches from across the street, and headed to my evening job. I worked at Eastside City Service from 6 to 9 every other evening and Saturday. Even with two jobs, I still ended up borrowing money from the national defense student loan program to pay the balance.

Several things happened during that year that had life-changing implications for me. The first is the experience I described in the chapter called "The Light". The second experience (which wasn't realized until years later) was in a speech class led by Mr. Ed Meyer. He never knew what candle he lit in my life. One of the requirements for this class was to pick a reading or poem and present it to the class. This was a very small group, so I didn't have a lot of fear getting up in front of everyone. My reading, which I almost memorized, was TS Eliot's "The Hollow Men." My instructor was so taken back by my performance that he had me stay after class to visit. He had no idea that such a presentation could come from within me. He encouraged me to pursue some career in public speaking. Of course, I totally rejected that idea completely at that time. I kept it in the back of my mind though and pondered it often.

Settling down to college life led to my third year of college to be better than the prior years. To save money, I moved into my brother's apartment with his wife. That worked out great for me, since we had home-cooked meals. Since my brother was a meat cutter, he often brought home aged steaks. They didn't look good but were really tender. I could not eat the brains and eggs he sometimes fixed. My mind is foggy if I ever paid them rent that year. Maybe I still owe something? Even my grades showed improvement. The first semester I got 1 A, 1 B and 4 C's, and the second semester I got 4 B's and 2 C's. A third major event occurred that would have dramatic effect on my career. Taking some psychology classes from Dr. Rosemont, I began to develop an interest in the field of Psychology. During one class, Dr. Rosemont was talking about major life experiences that have a dramatic effect on our lives.

He talked about the birth experience, marriage and career selection. I remember raising my hand to make a comment. After acknowledging me, I challenged his list of life experiences and mentioned he was forgetting the most important one. I said I believed that the experience of being born again outweighs all the others. He walked right up to my seat and leaned over me and said in a very emphatic voice, "Excellent, excellent, Mr. Weidner! A very important, very important point!" No further explanation was needed, because I could tell in his response he had first-hand experience with that. From that moment on, I could do nothing wrong in his class, and got all B's. Talk about teacher's pet!

Still needing money, I went to work for Dakota Welding. My job was to deliver oxygen tanks all over town to welding shops and hospitals. We used a pickup to deliver the tanks. In order to load the tanks, I would lean a 5 foot tall tank over my right knee and slide it in the pickup. These tanks were too heavy to lift all alone. In time, I began to experience extreme pain down my right leg. Further explanation regarding health issues will be cleared up later when I talk about medical issues. This ended my track career for good.

In my senior year, a resident hall director position open in Voorhees Hall, so I was able to get a free room for the year. They also needed someone to keep restrooms clean, so I took that job as well. During my first two years in college, my roommate was from Bryant, South Dakota and we hit it off very well. During year three I lived with my brother and now my senior year my roommate was my cousin Del Gross, who was more like a brother. What a wonderful year we had studying, eating popcorn, and drinking orange pop. Adding student teaching my final year kept me very busy. With my back becoming a serious issue, several of my grades suffered to the point I had to drop some classes. I did end up with 2 B's and 4 C's. In order to graduate with my class, I needed to attend both sessions of summer school. I was able to squeak out three

B's and 1 A that summer. I went through the graduation ceremony that spring and got an unsigned diploma. It was signed as soon as I finished summer school requirements.

Where was God?

Thrusting myself into this new, strange, and sometimes fearful environment, I often felt overwhelmed. The idea of being completely independent was not new to me, but I had no concept of time management. My mother encouraging me to stay in school and keep trying was a key moment for me, as well as when one professor seeing public speaking potential in me and another professor acknowledging me for my innovative thinking on things that have dramatic effect on our life. It seems that God was using people to help bring about His purpose in shaping me for His service. Praise God for candle bearers who were being used in small ways that later had a big impact on one insecure country boy. I am beginning to see that there were candle lighters in every phase of my life.

College graduation picture

21

Lessons Learned in College

As a sophomore, my classmates encouraged me to get involved with student government. That year they elected me as vice president of my class, and I also joined a Circle K group. Circle K is a college-aged group affiliated with Kiwanis International. My junior year, my class voted me as president and I was also vice president of Circle K club. During my senior year, I decided to forgo any class office since I was busy trying to keep up with classes and because of my illness. I was honored to be selected as a homecoming candidate for pow-wow days, along with two other classmates. Even though I did not get selected in the final vote, a valuable lesson was learned. I was told that my second place was only two votes shy of winning. If my best friend had voted, and I had voted for myself and not my classmate, the results would have been different. I learned a lesson that day to always vote for yourself.

As an officer in Circle K, I attended the national convention in Washington, DC, along with two others. There we were met by Carl Munt, the senator from South Dakota who showed us around the capitol. I had never been that far from home or taken such a long bus ride. Serving as a class officer and a Circle K officer gave me certain skills and a leadership ability I never knew before.

Even though Huron College was a Presbyterian school, there wasn't much opportunity for spiritual growth there. Realizing the need for something, I started a Bible study group. Out of that group came six students who later went on to be in full-time ministry. One embarrassing meeting for me was during communion when we ran out of the fruit of the vine. People were good and took some empty glasses to drink, even if it was just a drop. A lesson learned from that experience is to always prepare for more than you expect.

I was asked to be part of a group that traveled to different churches to conduct services. That turned out to be a real growth experience. My part was usually speaking, since I could not sing. One vivid memory was traveling to Sisseton, South Dakota. Driving around town, we finally reached a Presbyterian church. Inquiring inside, they said that we were not scheduled to be there and they didn't know of any other church. We did find a Native American Presbyterian church that didn't have a set starting time, so whenever people got there we planned to start. One of my friends had the sermon that day titled, "The Ecumenical Movement in Today's World." I'm pretty sure that it didn't go over very well for that particular church group. Many appeared quite confused over the topic. They had also planned a potluck dinner for us. At the time I was very fussy eater and didn't care for any of the Native American dishes.

Where was God?

My college years were transitional years when I learned to give up some of my old habits and learn new ways of behaving. The saying that old habits die hard was very real to me. Out of these experiences, God was teaching me leadership skills, speaking skills and skills in serving. I had no idea how God would use these different offices I held to mold me and to make me more useful for His service in the future.

22

A College Degree in One Hand/ Marriage License in the Other

My long-term goal was to get my BA degree before I ever got married. After finishing my summer school makeup classes, my diploma was finally signed on August 11, 1965. Naturally, there was no reason to wait any longer so that blonde and I were married on August 12, 1965.

It was during that summer I also signed a teaching contract which required me to be in Iowa ten days after the wedding. After meeting with one school in South Dakota, I realized that schools in Iowa paid much more. Dressed in my finest suit, I headed for my three interviews in Iowa. Mother had drilled into each of us to always look nice for work applications. Needing clothes for work, I soon realized my two brothers were also buying clothes for their work. By chance we all met at Osborne's clothing store where suits were going on sale. The salesman happened to be an area basketball official named Dave Johnson that knew all three of us. The sale special was to buy two and get one free, so we all walked out of the store that day with nine suits among us. Dave told a lot of people about the day he sold the Weidner Brothers all those suits. That day I had purchased a gray, blue and a maroon sharkskin suit. I think mother's advice paid off in my first interview.

Dressed in my new gray sharkskin suit, white shirt and tie and newly shined black shoes I was offered my first teaching job.

The only bad part was there wasn't much time to get married, have a honeymoon, get housing and be at school in 10 days. We found a two room apartment above the city liquor store on Main Street. My contract included teaching three classes in world history and one sociology class. Part of the contract required me to be an assistant coach in football, basketball and track. Boy did I regret being at school two weeks early for football, since I had never even held a football in my hand! I had zero knowledge of the game but eventually the head coach found my expertise was in taping ankles. I was privileged to coach a quarterback who later went on to the University of South Dakota, received his law degree, and became the assistant attorney general of South Dakota.

We chose our wedding day between the schedules of school, work, and our pastor's availability. Looking back we maybe should have put more weight on the possibility of high temperatures in August. It was very hot and uncomfortable on our wedding day. We got through the service and headed towards Yellowstone National Park. It was 10:30 at night as we were passing through Miller, South Dakota and realized we needed to rest. We stopped at a motel on the west end of town and I went in to get a room. Showing my youth, inexperience and just plain stupidity, I asked for a honeymoon suite. The guy at the desk could barely keep from laughing. We settled for a regular room. As I was getting ready to brush my teeth and go to bed, my wife was still in the bathroom. I thought maybe a little nudge to her to hurry was in order. In my attempt to open the door, I discovered it was locked. This did not look good for me but she eventually came out. For years we have laughed about that first night together. It was all good after that…no more locked doors!

My in-laws had just purchased a new Chevy four-door sedan without air-conditioning. With this car we traveled through the Badlands. The next day, the temperature reached 104°, so we purchased bags of ice to cool our feet off. All of our plans changed because of the heat. The rest of our honeymoon was spent in the Black Hills of South Dakota. Once again we showed our lack of experience by agreeing to spend two days in a pop-up camper with college friends. It sounded like a good idea at the time. The next three days we roamed through the Black Hills of South Dakota. Then it was back home to pack and to head to Iowa. With the '59 Chevy Impala loaded, along with the U-Haul trailer, we headed out for Kingsley, Iowa.

Where was God?

It seemed like a miracle being able to graduate with my class in spite of missing a lot of school. Everything worked out to attend summer school so I could complete the requirements for graduation. I believe there was a higher power in working out graduation, marriage plans and a new job all in a workable timetable in that one year. I think we were too busy during this time to realize God's hand in making everything possible.

Wedding Day

23

"I Wanna Go Home"

With the windows down and the wind in our face, we headed down the road to our new home. Each of us realizing a new life was in front of us, but also desiring to hold onto the old. We drove a while in silence thinking about the rushed life behind us and all the new things ahead of us. I decided to turn on our favorite radio station KOMA and listen to music. Wouldn't you know the first song up was a Bobby Bears 1963 classic "I wanna go home!"

Maybe a few tears fell as we drove further and further away from each of our homes. Neither of us had ever traveled very far from home for very long. The closer we got to our new home, the more we realized that everything would be new and that was scary.

We settled into our two room apartment as well as my new job. It wasn't long before the flu set in and my wife got very weak. I put a call into the local clinic to see about a doctor. They asked which one we wanted to see since we didn't know either one. They said one was very soft and quiet while the other was quite straightforward. We picked the quiet and soft-spoken doctor and they said he would stop by the apartment after hours. I didn't know doctors made house calls anymore. After taking care of my wife, we had a chance to visit. Much to my surprise, he was a Mennonite from Nebraska. From that moment on, he became our full-time doctor, delivered both of our children, and became my best friend for life. Later we became partners in a new church planting in our town. We spent many evenings planning and praying for this new work.

Where was God?

Leaving the place we have lived in for many years and traveling to a new and strange environment gave both of us some anxiety. Even though we longed for home, friends and all that was familiar, we were graced by new friends. Our new doctor and his family was a real God send. Being slightly older and very established, he gave us calmness and security we both needed. He not only became our doctor, but directed us to Central Baptist Church in Sioux City where we later joined and made good friends. The things we often worry about are already taken care of in God's plan for us.

24

Not Qualified

Sometimes events that appear to be the worst thing ever turn out for the best! Such is a case for much of my life. The state of Iowa rejected my teaching certificate for the second year due to my lack of education courses required by the state. The state did grant me a one year certificate, but required me to take more courses before my permanent certificate would be granted. The very last thing on my mind was more schooling. Since I was required to take more courses, I thought I may as well apply them towards a Master's Degree.

In order to enter a Master's Degree program, one must take the Graduate Record Exam to qualify. So in the summer of 1966, I took the exam required for graduate school. Knowing my grades 1-16 were terrible, I had no hope of passing to be eligible for any program. The graduate record exam records areas of aptitude in verbal and quantitative areas. Waiting for the results was like waiting for a death sentence, because my whole career rested on this test. I did not know the requirements needed for entry, but I was sure that my verbal score of 21% on the verbal aptitude and 61% on the quantitative aptitude would not make the cut. Even if I got in, what major would I take? Several things led me down the road I eventually took. With a BA in psychology, a growing need for school counselors, my colorful upbringing, unique life experiences, and my love to listen to others with problems helped me to know my path. After applying to the University of South Dakota School of Guidance and Counseling, and then hearing of my acceptance into the program, I was dumbfounded. Someone must've thought more of my ability to succeed than I thought of myself!

With new hope, I started my classes in Sioux City sponsored by the University of South Dakota. Over the next three summers along with several night courses, I concluded my program in the summer of 1969 with my MA degree in Guidance and Counseling. Several of my classes were from SDSU in Brookings, South Dakota, but I finished my degree at USD in Vermillion, SD. With a lot of God's help, guidance and direction, I was able to graduate with a 3.5 GPA.

Where was God?

In life we are told not to sweat the small stuff. On the other hand, it seems that our lives are made up of all the little things. I am reminded of the gestalt theory in psychology which says that the whole is greater than the sum of its parts. If we try and separate our experiences in life and try to explain each one separately, we fall short of what God wants us to become. God allows us to experience things not in their separateness, but in our totality. He sees our life in such a way that allows the individual events to come together to give meaning and purpose to our wholeness. In conclusion, my life is better, more complete, and God-honoring by having gone through a lot of trials and tribulations. Isn't it great that our God places road signs along the road of life? If we are looking, He is there as well as the signs from His Word.

25

A Mighty Move For the House of the Lord

Oh what joy there is when you have dreams and visions for what God might accomplish and it comes true! It took a while for my friend and me to see the possibilities of church planting in our town. Both of us had been driving to Sioux City to attend church for some time. As our friendship grew, so did our desire to have an evangelical work in town. Because of our weekly prayer time together, we heard of others who were interested in the same thing. When we got to the point of having 6 to 8 families involved, we set a time to start Sunday morning services. We were able to rent a building from a church that had combined with another church and had an open building for six months out of the year.

After a while there arose some difficulties that led us to pray for our own building. A portion of land opened up on the east side of town that we were fortunate to be able to purchase. Now the task began to figure out how we could get a building. We were very small and did not have much of a budget to go on. Suddenly we heard of a church closing about 15 miles away. After inspecting the building, we decided it would be great for our needs. With church approval and a few dollars in the building fund, we were set for the auction. As embarrassed as I could be on the day of the auction, I gave the chairman a check for hundred dollars to go to the building fund. When I arrived at his house that day, he informed me he had a medical emergency. Since I was the vice chairman, I would have to attend the auction to bid. The doctor's wife decided to go along and help me with the bidding. With checkbook in hand, and $737 in the account, off we went to buy a church. We had heard rumors that neighbors wanted to buy the building for a hog barn. Driving to the auction that day, I began to let doubt creep in, wondering how we could ever afford to buy a big 44'×75 foot building.

Before selling the buildings, the auctioneer decided to sell all of the contents. This put me in a real bind. We needed a pulpit and pews, but how would I know how much to spend and have enough for the building? Knowing the assertiveness of the doctor's wife, I was concerned with her interest in buying these things. The first things sold were the windows, screens and lights. With a little elbow to the ribs and a nod, I decided to buy the screens and lights. Next the pulpit was on the auction block and yes, I got a little nod to keep my hand up and bid. We now owned both items, but still had no building to put them in. The auctioneer started the bidding off for the building, but he got no bids. After lecturing us about the real value of the building, he opened up the bidding again with a very low amount. Bidding went back and forth for a while but the bid was not good enough for him, so he took a 10 minute break for everyone to think it over. During the break, we visited with some of the other bidders. They were surprised to find that we wanted it for a new church in Kingsley. Once the bidding opened up again, someone outbid me by few dollars. I didn't know how much money was left but I decided to bid one more time. I thought to myself, "I'll just have to cover the amount if we are short." The auctioneer pointed his finger at me and said, "Son, you just bought yourself a church." I was sitting in the pew trying to absorb this grand moment where God showed himself in a mighty way. Basking in the feeling of God's love toward us, I was rudely forced back to reality by the pesky woman who was with me. Somehow what she had to say was more important than my moment of glory with the Father. She couldn't wait to ask me if I knew how much we spent. I looked at her bewildered and answered, "Of course I don't have any idea!" I was slightly ticked off that she interrupted my moment with God. With a smile and smirk on her face, she blurted out that we had spent $737, exactly what was in the checking account! For me it was one of those moments when God's presence was real and I wanted to live in it forever.

To live on a mountaintop experience with Jesus is great, but that wasn't going to get our church moved to our new home in Kingsley. Coming down from that experience meant a lot of work ahead. We soon got a moving company from Hull, Iowa that agreed to move the building. What a joy I experienced the day they were ready to lift the church to slide the steel beams under. With four hydraulic jacks hooked up to a small truck, they slowly opened each valve that let oil flow to each jack that began lifting. I can still hear the building creek and groan as it rose off the foundation. My thoughts turned back to the day I sat in the front pew and the auctioneer told me we had won the bid. Loading it on wheels took a few days, but finally it came rolling down the highway. The Sioux City Journal heard about this and led with a front-page story with the headline that said it all... "It's a mighty move for the house of the Lord." My responsibility at the church continued as vice-chairman, deacon and Sunday school teacher. Our hope was that the church would be a beacon in the area with a fundamental church teaching.

In the spring of 1973, we experienced a lot of different obstacles in our path. My stepfather had gone through heart surgery in 1971 and was not doing very well. There was also dissent in the church with the pastor's wife. We finally made the decision to not sign a contract and we began plans to move home. Within 10 years of when we left that church, it was struggling internally with different power factions. Looking back, I now realize that any new church that draws people from different areas and backgrounds has divisions that arise. The pastor couldn't hold things together and soon left. Visiting pastors came in and were able to keep the church going for a while, but that too soon failed. Upon hearing this, my heart was broken. All I could do was let go of my hopes and accept reality. If nothing more than my spiritual growth came out of this, it was worth the effort.

It would be some 40 years later that the two original charter members of the church were able to regain ownership of the building. Dr. Hamm and I decided to gift it to a group of young people called "The Dwelling" who had been using the building for several years. Our understanding is that many area young people have come to the Lord and others have been deepened in their faith by this group. In spite of our absence, God's work continues.

Where was God?

I count this experience as one of God's marvelous works in my life. Through prayer, He brought a group together, provided a house of worship and provided resources to purchase land and buildings. Even though the church only lasted about 10 years, many lives were touched through our time together. Now the area youth are getting trained there to be God's leaders for the future. This was a mountaintop experience for me and God was right there beside me all the time. There is nothing as powerful as when you sense God's presence and His purpose.

26

Ron and the Peter Principle

Just because a person holds a piece of paper, does not mean he is ready to tackle the job itself. In every job I ever had, there was always a feeling of total inadequacy. The state of Iowa said I was qualified to teach all social sciences, even world history. They must have been unaware of my high school and college history grades of D's and Cs. My only hope was to stay a day or two ahead of the smart kids in class. Subjects like economics, sociology, and psychology allowed me some breathing room in the classroom.

Most people are familiar with "The Peter Principle." Contrary to the real meaning that says "people are eventually promoted to a point where they reach their respective incompetence", I always seemed to start there. After teaching two years and with two years of postgraduate studies complete, I was armed with a new certificate that qualified me for a counseling position. During that summer of 1967, a full-time counseling position opened in Clear Lake, South Dakota. I desired to get out of the classroom so this job sounded wonderful. I was only there one year as teacher administration conflicts made me desire to move on. Fortunately, the counselor in the school I left earlier had resigned his position. Knowing the school, kids and community made it easy for me to secure the job. Back in Kingsley, Iowa, we moved into the counselor's job and also bought his big house. After five years, we decided to leave and head back home. My stepdad was failing and he needed my help on the farm. We were also experiencing some trials in our friendships within the church. At the time they seemed insurmountable, so after five years I resigned my position. This was perhaps the second hardest decision we had to make in our life.

In the spring of 1973, we moved home and lived in an old farmhouse provided to us by a relative. Before moving, a position opened up in a small Christian school outside of Huron. At the time it seemed like that's where God was leading us, but in the middle of that summer, I received a call from my old college about a new college job opening. I thought nothing could be hurt by just visiting with them. Most of the staff remembered me graduating in 1965. The job was considered a federal position paid by the government and therefore the salary was very good and I was offered the job. Days of turmoil and confusion followed on what to do, since the salary was twice what the local Christian school was offering. The only wise thing to do was to seek wise counsel from someone who I trusted. This person was a fellow church member and a very successful farmer. In the end, I heeded his advice and took the college position. The job included being vice president of student affairs, placement director, internship director, student counselor, career counselor, director of human relations, cooperative education director, assistant basketball coach, the cross country coach and assistant to the financial aids director.

Since I had my summer free and there happened to be an old large barn on the farm, I started raising hogs right away. I purchased 10 sows from Mount Vernon, South Dakota. We no more than got them unloaded and they started to farrow.

At the college I settled into a nice office in the student center and my boss was a fine Christian man. Not only did I hold several titles, but my boss and I also taught a class called "will the real me stand up." It dealt with being self-aware and how we often show different sides of ourselves depending on our situation.

During this time I helped my stepdad out at the farm on weekends. There was always cattle work and feeding to do since he had his heart attack. During the last two years of his life, I did much of the farming and tending to the cattle as he was very weak. He never said how glad he was that I moved back to the area. His son told me after his funeral that his dad had expressed to him how glad that I was around to help them.

For years I have been haunted by that decision, wondering if it was the right one. How different my life might be had I not taken that new road! I think the salary being twice as much as the contract I signed led to this earthly decision. Looking back I now realize that the lack of prayer may have led to this hasty decision.

Where was God?

Life is filled with many decisions when it comes to where God wants us to serve. Where does God want me and on what road am I to follow? These are decisions each of us must make many times in our lifetime. Sometimes the allurement of what the world offers is too much and we succumb to it. Does God rule us out from ever serving or living for Him again? Certainly not, but some of the joy may be lost in serving because our way was not His first choice for us. A lesson I learned was take time to pray about every decision in life. Allow time for God to work out in your heart His leading.

27

Resigned Only To Be Fired

Getting fired is not something anyone looks back on with any joy or pride. Quite the opposite occurs most of the time. I wondered how this works when you actually resign, but get terminated anyway.

Oh, how the college had changed from the time I attended there 10 years earlier until my present employment! A new president can change the entire direction a college will take. It was no longer a Presbyterian Church-related school with a target of certain students. A whole new group of students were recruited from the South and from the Native American population. As Assistant Dean of Student Affairs, I saw firsthand all of the problems this created. Since I lived in the country, I dreaded receiving calls in the middle of the night from resident assistants about trouble brewing in the dorms. Two cases that stand out where when a student who had been drinking had a knife in the hall threatening other students. The other was when a resident assistant was coming home on his bike and a student jumped out from behind a tree and swung a golf club at him. Lucky for him, he was able to duck to avoid being hit. The administration resisted our attempt to expel the students. This occurred during the Native American movement in Minneapolis, Minnesota where bricks were being thrown at the courthouse during the Russell Means trial. One morning, I was startled by the beating of drums outside my office. We soon learned that the American Indian movement was on campus to put pressure on the president not to act harshly on any students. Going against our wishes, the President did nothing because he feared further trouble from the AIM group.

These events began to put my boss and me at great odds with the administration. To further complicate matters, I was raising feeder pigs where I lived and was selling them at the local market. The market owner was also on the board of trustees at the college. He often asked about things at the college and we told him of our concerns. One more area of disagreement occurred when the Dean required me to complete a job description for the US government. I felt the need to be truthful in listing all the jobs that I performed. Apparently, listing the one class I co-taught was in violation of the government's use of funds. No money was to be used for teaching classes. The college was having three of us on federal payroll to each teach one class, thereby eliminating one teacher salary for the school's payroll. I refused to sign the government report which omitted the one class I taught. If the report was sent in, it was without my signature. During my last meeting with the Dean of students he portrayed childlike behavior by tucking his legs under him curling up like a ball. He would then lash out at me by on curling his legs pointing the finger at me and yelling like a spoiled child. Leaving his office that day, I was stunned that someone with a doctor's degree heading up the college's academic program would display such paranoid behavior. After that day, I was fearful to be near him.

The Dean of students and I continued to put pressure on the President to dismiss some students for misbehavior. On occasion, my boss would accompany me to the local sale barn for meals. The owner would always ask us the question of what was really going on at the campus. We felt compelled to tell him how we really felt, and that had severe consequences for both of us. Another person who called and asked about things on campus was my family doctor Howard Saylor, who was also on the board. With negative information coming from two board members, the President decided that information given to two board members violated the normal chain of command in settling disputes. Armed with this new revelation, my boss was called to the President's office one morning and asked to sign the letter on his desk. This was his termination notice to be off-campus by 5 o'clock that day and not return with the exception to pick up his check once a month.

With my boss gone, I had numerous students in my office crying over what was happening. With a new student uprising, I decided this was not a place I wanted to continue to work. Hoping to continue to help students complete their search for employment, I resigned effective at the end of the school year. Arriving at the office on Monday morning, my secretary told me that the President wanted to see me right away. I entered his office and was directed to a chair, told to read the letter and then sign it. I was told to pack my office and be off campus by the end of the day. Having never been fired before, this was a terrible blow to my ego.

It took 30 years later for some of the things we saw that were wrong to take its final toll on the college. The door closed in 2005 because of financing. The college campus is now home to the Splash Central water park for the City of Huron.

Where was God?

I now look back on that experience as one of my great spiritual battles. Standing up for one's values no matter how much heat you take strengthens your faith. I moved forward in spite of being called an educated fool by one of my uncles and being threatened by my mother to be taken out of the will. (This by the way never did happen.) The great spiritual lesson it taught me was to always be truthful and faithful and He will provide.

28

Back To My Roots... a Disaster in the Making

When my stepdad passed away in February 1974, I had to step forward and help mother run the farm. Being back on the farm got me thinking about going back to farming full time. I felt the only fair thing to do was buy mother out. With the help of FHA, and a partial contract for deed with mother, we jumped in with both feet and bought all the livestock, machinery and land. The Farmers Home Administration was there to help young farmers get started. Even though they approved my loan application, there wasn't much optimism that I could be successful. We took off with great hope and expectation. Because of FHA's financial involvement, everything we did had to be part of our annual plan. Looking back, I now realize that perhaps I did not have all the skills necessary to run an entire farming operation. Even though I was raised on the farm, and helped my stepfather for several years, that did not fully prepare me to take over the complete operation. Because of their involvement, we had to run all checks through FHA and all purchases needed to be pre-approved. When our projected budget did not come close to our actual income, the burden fell on my shoulders to figure out what went wrong.

I would describe the next ten years of farming as a total disaster. The following is a partial list of bad things that happened:

1. In 1976 we had a complete drought with no crops harvested at all.
2. A winter blizzard was responsible for killing 24 calves out of our 75 cows.
3. Another drought required us to sell all of the cattle for a severe loss.
4. I had back surgery and we were unable to get all of our crops harvested.
5. We lost an entire quarter of wheat that was in windrows because of the continual rain.
6. Because of back surgery, spring wheat and winter wheat got mixed up in the bins and when we went to plant spring wheat we didn't realize it was winter wheat and we lost a whole quarter of wheat.
7. When we purchased a new 60' x 168' steel frame building, we were sent the wrong blueprints and a two-year lawsuit ensued.
8. To supplement our income, we purchased 400 steers from Montana and fed them through the winter only to have a market drop and end up with $50,000 in corn bills.
9. A severe fire caused considerable damage inside of a brand new hog barn.
10. While building a pit alongside our new hog barn, severe rains cause the pit to collapse.
11. During this time we developed a rare scour problem with our hogs and had a high mortality.
12. My wife had an accident with the pickup and horse trailer while hauling butcher hogs to market.
13. Our son had an accident with the gravity wagon and was nearly killed.
14. We planted 100 acres of cane for feed, only to lose most of it to the rainy season.

There are only so many financial blows a farmer can sustain in order to survive. With approval and encouragement from FHA, we tried new avenues to generate additional income. We built a new 30' x

100' hog barn to increase our hog production. We also constructed a large building that we thought would provide several benefits such as more grain storage, machinery storage and a shop area for maintenance. With one disaster after another happening, our spirits began a downward spiral. With a rejection for refinancing from FHA in the mid-80s, there was no daylight anywhere for us. Bordering on the brink of self-destruction and being drained of all hope, I realized there was no way out of this mess. Not wanting to go on, and realizing some decisions I made were risky, there was nothing left to do but to give up. Having prided myself in always making my own decisions, I now longed for some wise counsel. Why did I think I could make this work?

I had learned very little from my stepfather about farming, farm management and financial management. My trusty FHA advisor did give us some guidelines and told us to sell all the livestock and reduce our debt. At the point he suggested I get a larger tractor to do custom work and should consider either Allis Chalmers or an Oliver because they were cheaper, I then lost all faith in his counsel. As the walls continued to close in, I planned for the worst. For the first time in my life, I experienced a total drainage of all physical, mental, spiritual and financial energy. As a practicing Christian during this time, I couldn't help wondering where the church was in all of this. Looking back, I now realize the church was grossly inadequate and ill equipped as to what to do and how to deal with someone in this situation. The easiest thing to do was to do nothing. Maybe the church didn't know one of their members was standing on the precipice of a cliff ready to jump off. It's very unfortunate the church often looks at different situations and develops judgmental feelings about that person's predicament based on the things they saw happening. "If only he would not have done this or not done that, he wouldn't be in this predicament." I asked myself why compassion often takes a backseat to judgmental feelings.

Hope comes in a most unlikely form. The federal government realized the dire situation of family farms. A new program was passed by Congress just for financially strapped farmers. This new program allowed farmers to completely reorganize their debts and stay in business. Loans were provided at low rate of interest to help with operational expense. Thousands of farmers took advantage of the opportunity to keep farming. Reluctantly, we join the program and lived to farm another year because of chapter 12.

Several years into my reorganization program, the church did finally step forward, but not as I had hoped. My mother had passed away and we received a small inheritance from her estate. We decided to put the money towards a car for each of our children. After 10 years of terrible luck, and now three years into our reorganization, we finally get a visit from the pastor. I was thinking his visit was a little late, but I reasoned at least he is here now. It was a devastating blow to learn his visit was to inform me that the church board was very unhappy at my decision to purchase cars for my children because of how it looked. I was barely able to control my anger and rose to my feet to inform him that my mother had to die for him to come to me to render that judgment. For 13 years he never darkened my door to comfort us, but now he was coming with some kind of financial chastisement? I didn't think I could drop any lower emotionally, but this was a stake in the heart that left scars I still feel today. In spite of this experience, I went on to serve as Sunday school teacher, deacon and Sunday school superintendent in that same church for many years.

With the help of this new reorganization plan we were able to continue. God led in marvelous ways to provide much-needed income. With this new hope and optimism, we continued to move forward.

Where was God?

As things went from bad to worse, we did question our Lord. In the background He pushed, nudged, coaxed and pleaded us onward. Through every valley, we gained strength to go on and even experienced a few mountaintop joys. Going through these many tough times was like going through the fire. Not happy with each experience, but once through, we felt more purified. Adversity taught us not to focus on things, but to hold on to that which is eternal. A person could easily ask why God allowed us to experience so much. It's a good thing we didn't tell God "that's enough" because there was much more down the road.

29

Income From Nowhere

With the farm barely paying its own way, we needed a source of income to pay our living expenses. There were few options for a second job with a steady income while still allowing me to farm. What I needed was a job that I could work on my own time. Insurance sales seem to fit that situation perfectly. I passed the tests for life, health, property, and casualty and started to search for a job. It just so happened that Farmland Industries was starting a new insurance program for all local cooperatives. I was immediately given the job. My responsibility was to service all the employees at various co-ops, as well as sell insurance to those who belonged to the cooperatives. With a car, a fixed salary and all-expenses-paid, life went very well. Since most farmers thought highly of farm cooperatives, especially Farmland Industry, sales went very well. At the end of the first nine months, I earned a Caribbean cruise. I'm sure there were those people who were wondering how a broke farmer could be going on a cruise.

No matter how content we may be with our present situation, when new doors of opportunities open, we need to explore them. Most of the members of our local church had health insurance through our denomination. This program was called Mennonite Mutual Aid. Within each church, there was one member who took care of that church's business and did all the service work for the members. Their compensation was provided in the form of free health coverage for them and their families. Because of the increased complexity of the health industry, MMA realized the need for a licensed person to provide these services. Their plan was to hire a person to service all of the churches in one area. I was offered the job to take care of seven churches in central South Dakota. Most people desired to have all of their coverage with one person. This led me to get other companies in order to provide a full service insurance agency. Goodville Mutual was a company that provided car insurance and liability insurance to supplement MMA. This company was added to our portfolio, along with Protective Life Insurance. Since Goodville Mutual operated out of Pennsylvania, it was difficult to provide service to their agents in the three states of South Dakota, Minnesota and Iowa. After visiting the home office, they offered me a position of regional marketing representative for the three state area. My responsibility was to train all agencies about new policies, procedures and deal with any problems. I began my new job with a new car and compensation based on the hours on the job.

By this time my plate was very full with full-time farming, raising livestock, running an insurance agency and now serving as regional marketing director. In spite of the fact that farming was very rocky, we were blessed with a steady income to provide for our needs. During the 20 years of farming, we were able to maintain an independent insurance agency. My regional marketing director position lasted about three years until the company no longer offered insurance in these states.

Where was God?

For those of you who know God and how He works, you are probably saying that He always provides a way. Just about the time we are ready to give up, something showed up to get us through. People often use the expression "it just so happened," but that is not revealing the sovereignty of God and His power. With Christians, things don't "just happen." How much do we have to experience before we have complete trust and reliance on Him who provides for our every need?

30

The Lord Sends A Ladder

There is an expression that says "when you're in a hole, quit digging." Well, selling all our cattle and hogs to reduce debt did not get us out of the hole. Imagine our surprise when God dropped a ladder to us and told us to start climbing. The ladder was an idea that came to us out of the blue. Baby calves were being sold at the sale barn by several area farmers, so we started buying a few. A local colony instructed us how to keep them alive. Word soon spread that we were buying baby calves. A late winter storm came through causing farmers to bring calves inside the barn. One farmer could not get the mothers to claim the calves after the storm. He offered me the chance to purchase them and I only had to pay him for the ones that stayed alive. I loaded up 23 calves, who were all suffering from scours. I had chains to tie each calf to the wall with double rings with pails inside for each calf. Within one day, I had them all drinking milk from a pale and only lost two calves. We continued to buy until we had 65 calves. They were all sold the next spring. That little venture provided to us with some seed money for the next year.

A lot of farmers were beginning to plant sunflowers as a rotation crop. To keep weeds under control, they needed Teflon. I felt a prompting to buy a 42 foot Herman super weeder and put a 500 gallon tank on the hitch. With a little plumbing we attached spray nozzles and installed a PTO pump with pressure gauges to the tank. This machine had four rows of "S tines" and three rows of harrows or drags in the back. It sprayed chemicals as it lightly scratched the surface and then smoothed the ground with the harrows. A perfect seedbed was created. We hauled water with an old fifth wheel truck box with a 1000 gallon water tank on the bed. Later I added two belly tanks mounted to our 4840 John Deere tractor that added another 600 gallons of liquid. As more and more custom jobs came in, the further behind I got. Since I had a 24 foot field cultivator with harrows, I purchased a bulk tank on four wheels. After adding spray nozzles and another pump system, we went with two applicators. This was pulled by our 4630 John Deere and was driven by my father-in-law. My task was to keep everything rolling and supply water. I got up at 4 AM every morning to fill everything so it was ready to go at sunrise. We got water from the ditches or dugouts in various locations. To my amazement, we covered about 2500 acres that year. This generated sufficient income to keep on farming.

Since custom work was so good to us, I decided to expand to planting and harvesting. We purchased a 12 row 30 inch John Deere front fold 3 bushel hopper corn planter. In the best year, we planted several thousand acres of beans, sunflowers and corn. We added an all crop head for harvesting sunflowers so we could add more acres to our load. Several other combining jobs continued to come in during this time.

In my spare time, I began to weld things together. After I designed a large toolbox for John Deere combines, several orders poured in. I could never understand why JD never came with a bigger toolbox. Most farmers ended up throwing tools in the cab and they were always in the way. People with IH combines wanted to combine sunflowers, but were forced to buy a John Deere all crop head. Since the heads were different, an adapter was needed. A few orders for this adapter came in and I was able to build those.

Most farmers baled hay and straw and wanted to haul as many bales as possible. I designed a three point hitch bale hauler that would hold two bales outside and one stacked in the middle. When you put that on the back of a loader tractor, you could carry 5 bales at a time for stacking. My life went from not knowing if I wanted to go on, to not having enough time in the day. It was as if the Lord was saying, "You need help, and I am sending it." Perhaps He knew that the best thing for us was to keep busy, and we sure were. Between farming, insurance work, calves, custom work and building things for different people, there was not a spare moment. There was no time to feel sorry for ourselves.

Where Was God?

Opportunities that began to drop in our lap provided needed resources to keep us going. I continue to stand in awe of how God works in our busy lives. Regardless of how deep a hole we dig for ourselves, I believe we just need to ask for a ladder and then climb out with new opportunities God gives us. These new options may not be jobs we are used to doing, but we need to trust that God will give us ability to do them.

Custom Chemical Applicators/Raising Bottle calves

31

From Bad to Worse

How naïve we are as new Christians to think how wonderful life will be with sins forgiven and a newfound joy in life. Life was good after conversion, a new marriage and raising children. There were a few speed bumps in the road, but nothing earth-shattering. Life was tough on the farm. In 1985, we had the financial collapse. Three years later in 1988, my mother passed away, which only added to the emotional toll already taken on my spirit. She was the last link I had to my past and all hope of ever understanding the emotional toll she suffered was lost.

Another three years went by before another event occurred that altered our lives forever, and redirected our livelihood in yet another direction. A tiny mole in my wife's ear canal led to major surgery that would forever alter her quality of life. Undergoing a radical mastoidectomy that took 11 1/2 hours at the University of Minnesota Hospital, she was left with ringing of the ear and constant nerve pain. Now after 28+ years of numerous medications, the ramifications of that surgery still exists. After pursuing every conceivable medical option known, we fall back trusting God's wisdom and purpose. We now ask only for grace and strength to face each day keeping our eyes on Jesus our only consolation.

In 1994, we felt like the wind was gone from our sail. We no longer had the drive or energy to carry on. We decided to have a sale and rent out the land. A dream once held so tightly, seemed unimportant in the light of all that had happen. With the loss of my work partner, there was no way I could do all of the work alone. My wife amazed a lot of people and was able to perform the following tasks:

Running a large tractor to dig in fields and apply chemicals
Combining
Hauling grain with a grain cart
Hauling butchers to town with a fifth wheel or and backing up to the shoot with no trouble
Cutting pig's eyeteeth
Vaccinating pigs and calves
Castrating pigs
Scraping out manure from under crates
Running a farmhand loader
Driving a grain truck to town

Where was God?

Being in pain and sorrow doesn't indicate that God has forgotten us. God is where we want Him to be. If you push Him away and blame Him, He will step back but never far away. My prayer was always to have Him right by my side, even if I am in the fiery furnace. We need to call on Him and He will show us great and mighty things. Scripture says: "come unto me all ye that labor and are heavy laden and I will give you rest." Oh, how we needed refilling of our spiritual, mental, psychological and spiritual emptiness. Pray that God will fill your cup so it runs over.

32

A Tribute To My Mother

The story of my life would be nothing without my mother's story. She was born into an upper income family as the third child of twelve to Mike Hofer and Anna Gross on December 8, 1912 in Freeman South Dakota.

Isn't it interesting how two families that came from Russia could travel very different paths and yet later cross paths? While mother was being raised in Freeman, SD, the Weidner family (Ludwig and Matilda) had settled in the Delmont, SD area from 1919-1921. They came with two children and there had three more before leaving for Wisconsin. Both of my parents were being raised only 30 miles apart and never knew one another.

My grandmother, Anna Gross, was born in Olivet, SD in 1887. She later married Mike K. Hofer. Their first child Evelyn was born in Olivet. They later settled in Freeman, where grandpa ran the elevator and creamery business. During the next 15 years, 10 more children were added to the family. Edward was the next followed by Edna (my mother), Mary, George, Walter, Jake, Ruth, Sam, Melvin and finally Clarence. In February of 1928, after losing his business, Mike sold their house and a quarter of land near Frankfort, SD and purchased land north of Yale, SD. He loaded two trucks and headed for Beadle

County with wife and 11 kids. In 1929, the final child (Gracie) was born in Beadle County. My grandpa was always known as "Crippled Mike" because he had rheumatism in his hip. Later he developed tuberculosis in 1915, and had his hip bone scraped every day. As a result, his one leg was shorter than the other. Later in life, he was unable to work. My uncle George writes how his dad used to pass out from the pain as they tore open the incision every day to scrape his bones. There were times he was not expected to live.

Mother had just graduated from eighth grade in Freeman when her parents moved to Beadle County. Her dad had lost the elevator and creamery business when hard times hit the economy. Her folks were able to purchase 240 acres in Beadle County. After sitting around home for a year, she decided to do something. With no transportation to go to Yale, and no money for room and board, she caught a ride to Huron, South Dakota. Luckily, she found a place to work for room and board, so she enrolled in high school in 1930. After graduation from Huron High School in May 1934, at the age of 22 she enrolled in Freeman Junior College. During this time she earned her room and board at the John L. Hofer farm near Freeman. John L. Hofer hired mom's brother, George Hofer, who had developed an interest is his boss's daughter, Margaret. An agreement was made that mother would get a date for George with John L's daughter if he would get her a date with his good-looking friend named Abe Weidner. It worked out and both went on to get married. Upon completion of one year of study in May 1935, she took a teaching job in Ackerman School in Beadle County. Abe followed mother to Beadle County to find work. They were married after one year of teaching on October 25, 1936. One year later, in 1937, a son Quentin was born. Fourteen months later, in 1939, a son Larry was born. Mother only taught one year and then quit to raise a family. Less than two years after her second son, a daughter, Deanna, was born in 1941. Leaving the farm in 1941, they traveled to Racine, Wisconsin to find work. Because of family pressure, mother was baptized on March 8, 1942 in the St. John's Lutheran Congregational Church in Racine, Wisconsin. The whole family returned to Beadle County shortly after that. There her fourth child, Ronald, was born in 1943.

Hardened by the experience of losing her husband, she never showed much affection. Even though she never expressed her love for us no one ever doubted her deep concern. She showed her love to us through other ways, one of which was her cooking. Every Saturday, we came in the house about 3:00 to find the table covered with buns, caramel and cinnamon rolls, stritzel, bread and hunkeley, something like modern day kuchen.

She kept a clean house with scrubbed floors, and she ironed shirts. Our sister helped her with these chores and worked very hard. Just imagine for a moment five men coming in to eat fresh buns and minced meat sandwiches, caramel rolls, hunkeley and drink fresh farm milk. (Remember, we always left about a quarter of an inch of milk in the glass because of dirt in the bottom.) It took us many years to finally drink all the way to the bottom. Saturday was bath day in the early days and water had to be heated. There must've been a ton of clothes to wash. Mother insisted that our clothes always be clean. Our jeans had to be lined with wire frames so they would dry with creases down the front and the back. All shirts and hankies had to be ironed, thanks to my sister. Mother even went so far as to put small sachet packets between our shorts and undershirts so they smelled good. She did this with Avon perfume packets that she was selling.

Sundays were days of good food. Many times she made homemade noodle soup with fried potatoes and sauerkraut, and other days she served duck. As kids, we used to fight over the yolks she cooked from the hens that were butchered. In her later years in town, she always saved me some cooked yolks. Once when I was re-heating them in the microwave, she opened the door after hearing an explosion only to have one explode in her face! Many a good laughs were had over that experience.

If the saying is true that circumstances help build character, then she and I should have a mansion to hold all that character. Through it all, she taught us a lot, not by her words but by her life. I know few women who could have endured the obstacles that she faced and endured with such grace. No, she was not perfect, but none of us are. I think she did pretty well with all of us, considering what she had to work with. By losing two husbands, one child, raising four of her own and one stepchild, she showed us by her life the true spirit of endurance.

Where was God?

With perseverance and a tenacity seldom found, she took her faith to new heights. Humanly speaking, it would be impossible to have this life without a spiritual inner power driving you onward. I only know one place to obtain this kind of inner power and peace that carries a person forward. II Corinthians 4: 8-10 says, "we are troubled on every side, yet not the distressed: we are perplexed, but not in despair: persecuted, but not forsaken, cast down, but not destroyed: always bearing about in the body the dying of the Lord Jesus, that the life also of Jesus might be made manifest in our body."

Mothers high school Graduation picture

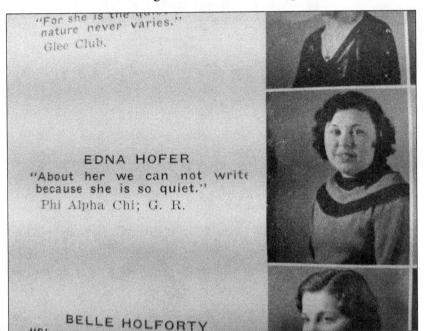

33

Getting the Cobwebs Out

Never having written anything of significance, the idea of writer's block was foreign to me. Midway through this book, something happened to me that I have difficulty explaining. In the beginning, I felt compelled to write my story, therefore it came easy. One day there came this emptiness of thought. I just couldn't get my ideas down on paper. I went to the Lord to seek help. "Lord, you called me to write, and now you are allowing my thoughts to swirl around in meaningless motion!" I cried out. This went on for about two weeks. Finally, the Holy Spirit spoke something in my heart. He said, "Get the cobwebs out."

I didn't know what that meant. Being a very analytical person, I looked at that phrase from a practical standpoint. What do we do with cobwebs in the house? The obvious answer is to get a broom, sweep and mop and throw them out. Okay, so I thought the next logical step was that I must look for the cobwebs in the far corners of my mind and sweep something out. Were there some things that I needed to get rid of and not speak about? God had a better idea. Those who believe that our Bible is God's way of speaking to us even today will understand how the mystery was solved:

Psalm 51:10: "create in me a clean heart o God and renew a right spirit within me."

Matthew 5:22: "but I say unto you, that whatsoever is angry with his brother without a cause shall be in danger of the judgment."

Hebrews 12:14: "follow peace with all men and holiness without which no man shall see the Lord."

Romans 12:18: "if it be possible, as much as lieth in you live peaceably with all men."

His Word had spoken, and now I must respond. Searching the dark corners of a checkered past led to several things long hidden. The revealing light of God's Word now brought these behaviors forward so they might be seen in the daylight. The Association of Bible counselor's website says "Christ likeness is inextricably bound to the health of our relationships." If our life is laden with broken relationships, how then are we to have healthy relationships with our heavenly father? What is our choice in life? We are to use the power of a sincere face-to-face apology and then learn to forgive ourselves.

With the mystery of my writer's block solved and task at hand, I set out to right some of the wrongs of my past by meeting with some people and writing others letters. The chains that tie us to our past can be loosened if we go through the steps and bring them before the Lord. How many of us are burdened by the chains of the past? Seek His forgiveness and the forgiveness of others to free up your spirit to have a closer walk with the Savior. Walking this road of life is so much better if we learn to walk closer to Jesus. The closer we walk, the more we desire to shed ourselves from past chains, present temptations or worrying about future valleys.

Where was God?

If anyone doubts the power of the Holy Spirit, they should examine their life a little closer. I have experienced His power in blocking my thoughts and redirecting my mind to things that need immediate attention before I can go on. For me, it was a training process to learn to look for and to listen to the leading of the Holy Spirit. This experience has burned in my memory the joy of looking for, listening to, and then following that calling. Beloved, if this is not something you have experienced in your walk, I pray you will seek Him today.

34

Candle Lighters

Recently I was watching a public TV show where the moderator asked his two guests the same question. The question was, "Who in your life would you say was a candle lighter?" I had never heard that idea before. The opposite thought has flooded my mind quite often, when I wonder why someone wasn't there in my early life to set me on a better path. No matter how much I longed for a strong, caring person to step forward, no one ever did. So I thought.

Throughout the writing of this book, this thought kept lingering in my mind. I've included a section at the end of each chapter called "Where was God" to highlight my search for my candle lighters. I thought maybe if I dug deep enough in each experience, someone might show up that fit that description. Imagine my surprise when I discovered God had sprinkled different people along my entire life's journey who have sown seeds and lit candles. Let me share a few:

1. A third grade teacher, Ellen Kleinsasser, taught me to memorize John 3:16, but to put my name in the verse. "For God so loved Ronald Weidner that he gave his only begotten Son, that if Ronald Weidner believeth in him should not perish, but have everlasting life." Although my heart burned with joy at the thought, I did not know Him yet.

2. A neighbor and friend, Jake Entz, invited my friend and me to attend Byron Bible camp on a Saturday night. We both went and had a great experience until I got the mumps and was sent home the next day. It was a great feeling how people cared about you, but I did not know Him yet.

3. An evangelist at James Valley Christian School held revival meetings one fall. Each night he had us say Jeremiah 3:33, which says: "call unto me and I will answer thee and show thee great and mighty things which thou knowest not." Ending one service, he called for all the young Christians to come forward. I went forward with my girlfriend, but I did not know Him yet.

4. During grade school, my sister and I attended revival meetings above the grocery store with Manny Wallman and Nelson Poe. My sister went forward at the call for salvation, so she dragged me up front as well. Kneeling around the small table during prayer, I elbowed my sister to ask what we were doing up there! After that, I loved listening to their music on Saturday morning on KIJV. Even though I was led forward for salvation, I still did not know Him yet.

5. A preacher I called a "Mexican jumping bean on steroids" got a hold of me and would not let go. During the service, he gave the call to come forward for salvation. Obeying the call, I went forward and at that point I finally knew Him.

If you look hard enough, you will find people along the way who sowed, some watered and some harvested in your spiritual walk. Listening to the Spirit during the cobweb chapter, I realized we need to also deal with the positives. In my quest to encourage my candle lighters, I found many were deceased. After finding out that a daughter of one of my candle lighters was only two blocks from me, I set out for a meeting. I wanted her to be encouraged by her mother's compassion for Scripture memorization and what it meant to me. One more person I needed to contact was very ill, so I went to the nursing home to express my gratitude for his life and his years of teaching. The next day, Brother Ben entered the presence of the Lord, so I was almost too late. I believe our candle lighters need our encouragement, and we need to do it before it's too late. If I can be a help to others, you can be as well. No matter the wattage of your bulb that is within you, use your light to shine in the dark corners of someone's life that needs hope.

Another candle lighter showed up early in my teaching career was my doctor friend Chuck H. His quiet controlled disposition was something I needed in those years. In the few short years we had together he taught me a lot not only by his words but mostly by the way he lived his life. By his example I became a much better person. To list all those who had an impact on my life would be too lengthy. For some, it was just a kind word and others showed they cared by their actions. There were many other men who had influence on me in my early experiences with the church. Even now, I continue to find people who are inspiration and encouraging to me as I hope I can be to others.

Where was God?

The beauty of how God works is that you may not know Him or His involvement in your life. Just as He was leading, coaxing, and pleading with me to follow Him, He is doing the same with you. Now that I can say I really know Him, the veil has been lifted from my past and His constant presence is now fully realized. Look around you and you will also find candle lighters in your life. I found my candle lighters in the lives of Jim K., Butch, Walt G., Sam W., Jimmy H., Jake E., Sam T., Elmer G., Raymond H., Pastor Hofer, and many others who taught the Word in Sunday school while others' lived lives I admired.

Special thanks to dear friends who helped guide us through some of our darkest times and were always there for us. All the years we worked together were some of the richest times in my life. Thank you Norman and Deloris for being candle lighters in my life. Many of the people are now gone that never knew of the effect their life had on mine. May we all live life being candle lighters.

Norman and Delores Hofer, Ron and Paulette Weidner with son-in-law Keith Ulvestad

35

A Room Full of Tears
I Never Cried

Several years ago I was awakened from a deep sleep. I was told to write down the above words. Confused but obedient, I wrote this phrase on a yellow notepad. For years my mind searched for some meaning and purpose to these words. After searching for so long, I gradually began to forget about it. This happened somewhere around the birth of my first grandchild.

My job as an insurance adjuster required me to be on the road a lot. My territory was the entire southeast quarter of the state of South Dakota. These long trips provided plenty of opportunity to reflect on things. I began to focus on my new grandson and my love for him. How is it that a person can fall so deeply in love with a new baby in an instant? While others debated who he looked like, and was he cute or not, I just continued to love him. Somewhere along life's way, I was confronted with the realization that every newborn has a soul and will spend eternity in one of two places. As a new grandparent, this weighed heavily on me. I committed myself to doing everything in my power to steer this new life to Jesus Christ. There was abundant help in this endeavor because he had parents, two sets of grandparents, and many close uncles and aunts. I couldn't help think how lucky he was. Why was he so lucky to be so loved by so many?

There were many times as I traveled down the road, thinking about these things, that the tears began to flow. Often times I needed to pull over to wipe my eyes. After this happened a few times, I began to wonder if I was going crazy, but then I realized it was just because I loved my new grandson so much, it brought me to tears. This should not be happening to someone who has a BA in psychology and an MA in counseling. Perplexed and confused, I carried on with my work. Frequently I went through the list of people who surrounded my grandson with love, advice and encouragement. Finally the frustration over this whole matter began to arouse the anger within me, and I blurted out to myself, "why didn't I ever have one person show me the kind of love he gets?" Then it hit me that tears were now shed not just for him, but were mixed with the years of unshed tears of self-pity and loneliness.

My life had been lonely, full of loss and loveless. Growing up, I never realized what I was missing. Seeing someone else reap the desired fruits of love and acceptance began a hunger deep in my soul. What memories, feelings and emotions were stored in the deep corners of a young mind that were thought to be long gone or never known to exist and lying dormant? It appears there was a powder keg of anger long forgotten lying hidden. I couldn't get past it without God's help. We say that when Christ comes into a person's heart, He can heal all things. Heal yes, but what about the emotional scars left behind? Some psychologists say that if we failed to learn certain things in the proper time frame, later learning becomes difficult. Does this principle apply when love and affection are lacking at a young age? Years of scars are not healed by one big cathartic episode. This newly discovered room that is bursting with potential tears is now slowly being defused by daily commuting with a Heavenly Father by shedding a tear at a time. Looking back on life, there is always the sorrow of "what might have been". No one person is to blame, and certainly not my mother. Each of us is required to make the best of life, regardless of what we go through, even if we are living in the school of hard knocks. With me, it's still one day at a time, shedding one tear at a time.

Where was God?

It took a long time to learn to listen to the spirit of God speak to me. If you do not understand right away, give Him time to reveal to you in His time. Continue to listening to Him, even if it takes many years (as it had with me.) God used the life of a small baby to teach a grown man how to look inward and to begin to find peace. With each new grandchild, I gained a deeper love for each and so I live, hoping that they never experience that long lost, lonely, loveless feeling that I lived with for so many years.

The Original Title written in the middle of the night

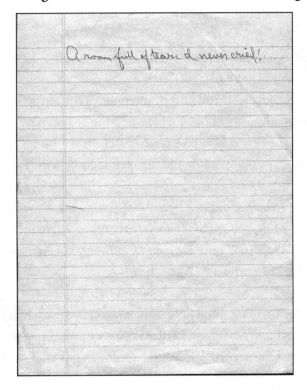

36

When the Body Cries Out

Is there anything in life that prepares you for pain? I guess the reality is that one pain prepares you for the next. How do you react to pain in your life? Much of what I have been sharing involves all kinds of pain, except physical. This could include psychological pain, spiritual pain, emotional pain and even economic pain. Intermingled with these pains I have endured, I also have a history of physical pain.

Going to a new doctor always requires a list of current medications you are taking and a list of all surgeries you've had. At this stage in life, it is much easier to hand them a list of meds and a list of my 36 surgeries. There are two lessons in life I wish someone would have taught me earlier on. The first is how to learn to listen to the Holy Spirit as He speaks to us. I wish it wouldn't have taken so long in my life for me to experience this. One of the reasons we miss Him speaking to us is that we just get too busy living our lives and we fail to take time to meditate. We are more easily touched when we are still and able to receive His prompting. Perhaps my illnesses were God's way of forcing me to slow down and listen to the moving of the Holy Spirit.

A second lesson is we often ignore the messages our body is trying to send to our brain. Messages are often dismissed as minor annoyances with no real significance. Ignoring the minor signs seldom solves the real problem, and almost always leads to more intensity of pain. If there are degrees of pain, I would be awarded a PhD. Let me share a few of the many courses I took on the road to this degree. I share these moments not as a source of piety, sorrow or attention to self, but so that you might see the mighty hand of God moving.

37

Health Issues

A. Appendectomy and a Confession.

I sailed through all of my early surgeries with no serious consequences. This included tonsil, appendectomy and blood poisoning in my knee. However an incident occurred during my hospital stay recovery from appendix surgery. It must've been my stepdad that checked me into the hospital. Since he was Catholic it was only natural for him to put that down as a religion of choice. I was not aware of this until much later. Close to the time of my dismissal the nurses asked if I was interested in taking communion. That sounded reasonable to me since I was 13 or 14 years old. A divider was wheeled into my room to separate me from my roommate. It was just a little surprise when a Catholic priest walked in but since this was a Catholic hospital I didn't give it much thought. I thought he was probably just making routine rounds. Approaching me and getting very close to my face made me a little bit nervous. Just then he reached inside his robe and pulled out a small microphone and shoved it close to my mouth. In a very low somber voice he said; "I will now take your confession". It took a few moments for me to process what just happened. I was thinking to myself that I have never confessed my sins to anyone let alone a priest. Why was he asking me for my confession anyway? Did someone tell him I was a bad boy and needed to confess something? Finally the brain freeze left and

I realize what must've happened. I said to the priest I am not Catholic but my stepdad is one. The look on his face said my God how did this mistake happen. He was so sorry for the imposition and left immediately. As the nurses came in later they teased me about my mix-up with the priest. For years I have wondered if all the priests have that little mike ready to hear a confession at any time and was it being recorded. I never did find out if true. Years later I thought maybe I should have told him some of the wildest most sinful things I could think of to see him react to my wild life. Thank goodness reason prevailed and it did not happen.

Where was God?

I could be wrong but I think God has a humorous side and he probably got a chuckle out of this situation. At the time I was not even a member of our Lutheran church and had never taken communion before. I had heard our church used real wine so I thought this was my chance to get a drink of real wine.

B. Used and Abused

Growing up on the farm, I never wanted to give up on any task I was confronted with. Nothing was ever too heavy or too difficult to tackle. My mentality was that I could put my mind to something and back it up against all obstacles and win. Pain and discomfort was a poor substitute for giving up. Many of the jobs on the farm required more strength and stamina than humanly possible such as digging post holes, pulling hay out of a frozen stack, hauling manure and picking rocks.

After delivering oxygen tanks around town while in college my toes began to tingle. I was a tough country boy so I didn't listen to my toes. Soon a strong message was heard from something down the back of my right leg. This pain felt like it was going to blow the ends of my toes off or even my kneecap. Wow I heard that! I tried many different remedies that people offered as solutions, but none of them worked.

A Sioux Falls doctor concluded my pain was coming from my back and not my leg after he did a myelogram. A ruptured disc was the diagnosis. I had surgery planned at Sioux Valley Hospital, but the night before surgery, the doctor found some pimples and immediately canceled the surgery. Later we learned that this same Dr. Vandermark had a brother who contacted osteomyelitis from a pimple that left him with severe bacterial infection. I decided to go to the Tschetter Hohm Clinic and see Dr. Tschetter. Late on a Friday afternoon, he heard my story and then got right on the phone and talked to a doctor in Minneapolis. As he hung up the phone, he said we were to be in Minneapolis, Minnesota on a Sunday afternoon because my surgery was scheduled for Monday morning.

Nine days later on June 13, 1964, I walked out of the hospital pain-free. Over the next 14 years, I gradually forgot the doctor's warning about not abusing my body. Once again my toes reminded me to stop tearing into things with little thought of how it would impact my body. In 1978, I was right back at the University of Minnesota Hospital for my second laminectomy. Thankfully, because of new lifting techniques, and a new mentality, my back has survived for over 40 years without further complications.

Where was God?

It's easy to wonder why it took so long for us to find a solution to my back problem. One of the early solutions presented did not set well with me. Spinal fusion was the surgery of choice at that time. This would involve a bone fragment placed alongside the vertebrae until it fused together. The patient would have to be placed on a striker frame that would spin so you would only be able to look up or look down. No movement of any kind was possible. Being slightly claustrophobic, the thought of being tied down for six weeks of healing would not have worked. Even though there were weeks of suffering, I believe God had something better than spinal fusion in mind. Isn't it true that God always has something better for us if we would just trust Him?

C. Dying Inside

One morning around 5:00 I was awakened by knife-like jabs inside my body. I was having sharp pains like I had never experienced before. I was thinking, "If this is death, it couldn't come fast enough!" We managed to get to the doctor's office but there was nothing he could do to dull the pain. Once admitted to the hospital, we needed a urologist as we suspected a kidney stone was causing the trouble. Given it hadn't passed on its own, and the pain prevailed, we knew we had to try something fast. First, doctors entered from below to try to find, snare and remove the stone. After that unsuccessful attempt, they next came through my back attempting to grab and remove that stone. That attempt was also unsuccessful. After enduring five more days of pain, my only hope was to get to the nearest lithotripter machine, which at the time was at the University of Iowa in Iowa City, Iowa. My mother hired a plane and sent us on our way. After checking into the hospital we learned that the machine was open the next day. In order for the machine to crush the stone, its exact location had to be pinpointed in the body so the sound waves sent into the body can break up the stones. Much to my disappointment, and for reasons that are still a mystery, the procedure was canceled. We assumed that maybe the plane ride had caused the stone to move and get stuck in the only spot in the body were the machine could not reach to crush it. My roommate in the hospital had just gone through kidney surgery, so I could see that was not something I wanted to endure. I was sent home with a port installed on my side and wearing a bag. The doctor hoped that by putting a valve on the line to the bag, we could possibly force the stone out the natural way. We were all hooked up and ready to go home, but we had no transportation home since we had flown to Iowa.

My brother had driven in from East Lansing to be with my wife throughout this ordeal. The hospital gave us the name of the church that often helps people with needs. Sure enough, they provided an apartment for them to stay at and had even loaned them a van to travel around the city with. Since my brother's pickup was too small for the three of us to go back home with, the church said to go ahead and take the van. All of us were strangers, but their trust in us was unwavering. It would have been a long drive for my brother to get us completely home and then back to Iowa City, so a fishing buddy came to our rescue. He agreed to meet us at my brother's home in Pocahontas, Iowa, and take us home from there. Larry headed back to Iowa City to return the van to the church and then back home to Michigan.

Back home, I continue to shut off the valve to put pressure on the stone to move. Day after day I tried enduring as much pain from the pressure as possible, only to give up. During all this time, we were required to strain the urine just to see if any stones were passed, but even that proved useless. After about two weeks, I told my wife I thought I felt something strange inside. With nothing in the urine that day, I gave up on the straining. The next morning I headed for the bathroom to go like every other day. All of a sudden, I heard a clink that was loud enough that my wife heard it in the kitchen. Running into the bathroom she said, "Is that what I think it is?" Sure enough! I had given birth to a small, snail-like stone the size of a match head. How could something so small cause so much pain for so long? I think we even celebrated the occasion that night.

Where was God?

Even a blind person could find God's handiwork woven throughout this ordeal. We may not have seen all His blessings during the pain, but looking back, I am humbled by the workings of His hands. Things just do not fall together like they did without a Master Planner. If you are in one of the storms of life, look for God's sunshine and His handiwork to break through at any time. What He did for me, He will do for you, as the song goes. This church in Iowa City was doing a tremendous work for people coming to the hospital. The Lord had made prior arrangements for my wife and brother to have a place to live and a car to drive. People say things just happen, but I don't really think so. God always has a plan.

D. A WALKING DEAD MAN

Because of my wife's prior surgery that left her with constant nerve pain, we were visiting the Mayo Clinic in Rochester, Minnesota. While she was seeing several doctors, she suggested I get a physical checkup. Anyone who has been there knows that you cannot just walk in and get an appointment. They have a process whereby you can fill out all the forms and you can wait in the lobby to see if any doctor has time to see you. For three days, I sat waiting until the final appointment at 3:30 was called in. Finally, at 3:00 on the third day my name was called and an appointment was confirmed for the next morning.

While in her office the next day, I asked the doctor what made her choose to see me out of all the people who were trying to get in. The power of the Holy Spirit was revealed to me as she explained that something inside of her directed her attention to my name on the list. She saw that I was a farmer, insurance agent and a Yale graduate. I didn't tell her until much later that it was only Yale High School that I graduated from, but at least it got me in to see her. A lot of the tests were lined up for me that day. The very first was a stress test to check out my heart. My wife said that I would breathe quite heavily after climbing the stairs, but I never thought anything about that. My first test was on the treadmill where I walked with wires all over my body. After about 90 seconds, they shut down the machine and informed me they were taking me to the heart doctor right away. I had heard rumors that Mayo Clinic was a no-nonsense hospital, and I soon found out that was true. The doctor was barely in the room before declaring, "Mr. Weidner, you're a walking dead man." These are not the words you want to hear so early in the morning (or anytime, really.) He continued to pour gasoline on the fire by explaining something serious was going on with my heart. I had to stay over the weekend and exploratory surgery was scheduled for Monday morning.

Monday's surgery included placing stints in the areas where blockage was occurring. One blockage was 98% and the other was 92%. With that amount of blockage, a heart attack could happen at any time. They called my condition a degenerative heart disease and warned me that I would most likely experience more trouble down the road.

How right they were! Since then, I've had three more procedures with stints inserted each time. I also had a pacemaker and defibrillator placed under my skin to help regulate my heart. I have been warned that if my heart stops, it will emit a shock to get it started again. Since I have never had a heart attack, and never used a nitroglycerin pill, getting shocked was now my only hope.

Later, while at another doctor visit, I was explaining a problem I was having with my left hand and dropping things. My orthopedic surgeon said it sounded like a carotid artery problem. In all my years of heart trouble, no one had ever mentioned my carotid artery. He insisted I do something immediately. That afternoon, my family physician scheduled an exam at the hospital. Within a few days, a doctor called and asked that I see him right away. The tests showed 100% blockage in the right side of my neck and 60% on the left. Surgery was scheduled ASAP because there was more blockage than previously diagnosed. Nothing could be done with the side that had 100% blockage, but the other side was cleaned out after determining that it was actually about 70% blocked. The doctor said a stroke could have easily happened with this kind of blockage.

So the walking dead man is still walking, thanks to God's intervention on both occasions. He surely must want me to get this book written. Armed with several heart medications, my life is now filled with new energy and optimism.

Where was God?

Isn't it great that we are given the privilege of looking back at life's struggles to see God's hand working? His timing and coordination of events and people cause me to be in awe. Skeptics would call this luck, chance, or just good fortune, but for those of us who know the Master of the universe, there is no such thing as luck. Ecclesiastes 3:11 reminds us, "He made everything beautiful in His time."

E. Sleep Driving

I strongly advise that if you are sleeping, you also should not be driving. Unfortunately, as strange as it sounds, I did this on four or five occasions. It truly is a miracle I traveled this road for so long without having an accident.

It started simply enough, with the occasional complaint from my wife about my snoring. I brushed that off as mere exaggerations. With time, reality sets in as others join in the chorus. Sleeping in a tent on the banks of Hell Creek along Lake Winnipeg in Canada, I was confronted by my growing problem. Those who were in another tent about sixty feet away were complaining of noises coming from our tent. My idea to solve the problem was just to get up and go fishing at five in the morning. Great solution!

On another occasion while sleeping in a motel in Pierre, South Dakota with my fishing buddy and his son, my snoring proved to be too much for them so they spent the night sleeping in the van. In spite of the pillows flying my way all night, I never missed a wink of sleep.

After driving in the ditch on four or five occasions, the problem became real to me. Driving 80 mph in the ditch headed towards Chamberlain one day, I suddenly hit a bump, woke up and soon realized that I was headed for a guard railing. Hitting the railing would cause me to plunge to the pavement below.

Traveling north of Yale one day, I was heading to the farm to mow the yard. I was pulling an enclosed trailer with a brand-new mower inside I suddenly realized I was in the ditch. I didn't want to suddenly turn the Escalade back on the road, which would have caused everything to rollover, so I turned farther into the ditch and then angled back on the road, missing the culvert by a only few feet.

Traveling to East Lansing with my pickup one year, I suddenly woke up after falling asleep driving. After pulling to the side of the road, a car pulled up beside me. A gentleman came to the window and asked if I was okay. He said they were following me for five miles, watching me travel from ditch to ditch waiting for something terrible to happen. He thought maybe I was having a heart attack. Resting for a short time, I took off and proceeded to drive straight through to Michigan.

Falling asleep while on the phone talking to my brother began to be a new normal. This was the last straw for my wife, so she insisted I do a sleep test. During the test you are hooked up to a lot of machines. Within five hours, the staff woke me up because of the level of noise coming from my room. There was no question that my sleeping habits were a real problem. They had recorded 168 interruptions in that five hour period. This included both breathing stops and self-awakenings, which were off the chart. The only answer was a CPAP breathing machine. Because the mask covered both my mouth and nose, I frequently tore it off in my sleep as it felt like someone was trying to smother me. The doctor recommended I try surgery to avoid the mask. I must not have been listening when they explained what the uvulopalatopharyngoplasty (UPPP) surgery would involve. They would remove that uvula, soft palate, tonsils, adenoids and any loose skin in the throat. Waking up with stitches all over my mouth and throat was a terrible experience! Not only was it a horrible surgery, but it never worked. Back on the CPAP machine I went, with a pillow nose piece that I still use today after 20 years. My machine is something I never leave home without.

Where was God?

God's hands were certainly on the wheel of my car on several occasions. Even though I do not fall asleep now while driving, I still want the Lord riding with me every mile I travel. Sleep now generates unbelievable energy I never knew before. Once on that CPAP machine, I would never want to be without it. Why is it that we so often fail to realize we need something or someone to help us with our problems?

F. Orders to Unplug All the Machines

Anyone who has been around me for very long has heard me use the phrase, "I have fire in the hole". You see, I have an acid reflex problem. TUMS was my pill of choice to put the fire out. Through the years, the TUMS became less effective, and I had an upper endoscopy. This showed I had a precancerous esophagus, and needed a daily dose of Nexium to keep the fire out.

After several years, I developed a severe pain in my lower left side. This was soon diagnosed as diverticulitis which is caused by pockets in the colon. Antibiotics will calm the infection down, but eventually the pain is too great and too often. Removal of the damaged section is the only permanent cure. I was told the procedure could be done by scoping with no incision necessary. Upon waking up after surgery, as I was reaching down to my stomach to feel where the intense pain was coming from I soon realized the large incision that was made. I was told scar tissue from prior surgeries made scoping impossible. Because of several complications that arose, I was in severe pain. This included kidney infection, bladder infection, a double hernia, four days of non-stop hiccups, pneumonia and a fever. Special doctors were called in to fight all of the multi-faceted complications I was experiencing. It was during this four day long struggle that I told my wife to pull the plugs on all the machines because I couldn't take any more pain. Well, you know women... they never listen to their men. Later on, I was quite glad she didn't. Right after my darkest hour, relief began to come. My pain turned to joy as I quit focusing on myself and instead focused on Christ and how He suffered. I have now learned to focus on His suffering and not my own. Many times I have walked through the valley of pain. The mountaintop experiences with Jesus afterwards erase all memory of any suffering I experienced.

Where was God?

Every time I find myself on my back in the hospital, I look up at God and say, "Well here we are again Lord, what are we going to work on this time?" What do I need to do to have a closer fellowship with You? It is usually the same answer related to giving up more of the things that would tie me to this world.

G. THREE TRIES TO GET IT RIGHT

Most people would consider themselves lucky to go 70 years with no broken bones. Coming through all the near tragedies in my life, I find it remarkable that I had never broken a bone.

There was only one thing left to do before my first trip ice fishing in the New Year. My ice auger had old gas in the tank, so I stepped out the back door to drain it. A very light snow had fallen that night, so everything was lightly covered in snow. Three steps out the back door and everything went flying. I remember holding the auger away from me so I wouldn't get gas on myself. Never in my life have I fallen so fast, with no chance to soften the blow. A small amount of ice had formed underneath the snow that caused me to go down hard on my right hip. My cell phone was on the workbench charging, so I could not call for help. Crawling inside on my left side, I drug my right leg until I was able to reach my phone to call my daughter. Since the shop is 50 feet long and I was 10 feet outside the shop, I had to travel about 60 feet. To describe my pain on a scale of 1 to 10 would not do justice to what I was feeling.

Finally the ambulance came, but they had trouble getting me on the gurney. On the way, I was sure they stopped at every light while not sounding a siren. While in the x-ray room, the nurse picked up my leg to get a better picture of the hip. I just about flew off the table in pain. Heading back to the ER, the nurse hit the side of the door with the bed that caused more pain in my hip.

It was decided I should go to Sanford Hospital in Sioux Falls for my surgery. Four stainless steel self-tapping screws were used to hold my hip together. The doctor said he would normally use three, but since my bones were so good he decided to put 4 in just for good measure. I was sent home to begin therapy in a few days. During therapy at home, I experienced a lot of additional pain and felt like I was walking downhill. Even after moving to Pro PT, therapy it was very painful. It took several weeks to get to the bottom of the problem.

One of the four screws had worked its way beyond the ball and was protruding into my socket. Within the hour, I was in surgery and a mere four and a half minutes later, I was in the recovery room. The one screw was backed out and my incision was glued shut once again. I was sent home to do 30 days of continual therapy. Before two weeks were up, the pain was unbearable again. On a Sunday afternoon, I packed my bags and announced my intention to head for the Sanford ER to check in. As soon as I checked in, they took me to a room where I finally got a PA to talk to and explain that I was not leaving without a new hip. I told him they could call the police, but I wasn't moving. Finally my doctor's PA arrived and gave me no assurance that the screw didn't scar the cup inside my hip. He explained that if it was scarred, it would never heal. "That's enough!" I said. I demand a new hip. A few moments later, he came back and said I was on the schedule for the next morning. Three days later I went home with a new hip, and never had to do one day of therapy. The only downfall was that I had a large scar and some numbness in the leg muscles, but I was pain-free. It's amazing how the doctor was able to adjust my leg to be the proper length so that I could walk correctly.

Where was God?

In the weeks following this experience, I received a lot of advice on how I should pursue resolution with that doctor, to make him pay for what he did. The hurt I saw in the doctor's eyes told me he was sorry for what had happened. He said that in his 18 years of repairing or replacing hips, nothing like this had ever happened. In spite of all that I suffered, I would find no joy in punishing him for a simple mistake. God gave me the grace to let it all go and to forgive. Earlier in my life, I would not have had the grace to let this go. God's continual forgiveness for my mistakes helps me to treat others with the same grace.

38

What I Have Learned From A Higher View

In reflecting back over my life, there was a lot of pain, suffering, sorrow and personal shortcomings. Even though we did get a bum start in life by losing our father, someone did come along and took us in and amply provided for us. I would like to think that with every bad situation something good comes along.

By zooming out and looking at life from above rather than on the ground, we can see how God used this life-altering event to make us kids all better people. We were all forced to work on the farm and learn things we would never have known in the city. Most of us did not like the work at times, but now realize the true valuable lessons learned. Unfortunately our stepdad never became a real dad to us, emotional bonds were lacking, but we managed to get along fairly well. We did manage to have a few good times over food, visiting with neighbors and evening card games. We played a lot at whist, canasta and even double canasta. Good times were always had over some homemade ice cream. I was lucky and I usually got to lick the inside beater.

When I reflect on my many personal shortcomings, I can see how all my deficiencies existed for my own good. Even the Apostle Paul in Second Corinthians 12:9- 10 boasts of his limitations. But we are reminded, "...

my grace is sufficient for the: for my strength is made perfect in weakness. Most gladly therefore well I rather glory in my infirmities, that the power of Christ may rest upon me. Therefore I take pleasure in infirmities, in reproaches, in necessities, in persecutions, in distress for Christ's sake: for when I am weak then am I strong."

It is through weakness that the power of Christ can be brought to light. Every shortcoming and limitation we have is a source where God can show Himself through us, if we allow Him full control. I have been blessed by having been provided so many opportunities in life through personal shortcomings, sicknesses, surgeries and normal occurrences of life... but I'm sure they did not all lead me to show others to Christ. Yes, I did get stronger as more things came my way, as the faith in my cistern got fuller and fuller. There were many times in the eye of the storm that I did not display the finest qualities of a Christ-filled life. At last, I can now say that through it all, I have learned to trust and obey as the songwriter so eloquently described. With affirmation, I can now say with Paul that I glory in my infirmities that the power of Christ may rest upon me no matter what life throws my way.

Slowly, I am beginning to realize what God is trying to teach each of us through trials and suffering:

1. <u>So that God may show us how to want what he wants</u>. James 13 says, "know this, that the trying of your faith worketh patience." We always need to remember that He came to be like us, so that we could become like Him. It is not my will, Lord, but your will in my life.

2. <u>So God may motivate us to follow Him</u>. Hebrews 5:8 says, "though you were a son, yet learned the obedience by the things which He suffered." If our suffering does not bring us to our knees, remember God is patient and will eventually succeed.

3. <u>So that we might be a comforter to each other</u>. 2 Corinthians 1:4 says, "Who comforteth us in all our tribulation, that we may be able to comfort them which are in any trouble?" Because of my 36 surgeries, I seldom meet someone who I cannot relate to in their suffering. People who suffer often have deeper bonds and the door to sharing the good news is often opened.

4. <u>To keep us from doing our own thing that could hurt us</u>. 2 Corinthians 12:7 says, "There was given to me a thorn in my flesh the messenger of Satan who buffeted me, lest I should be exalted above measure." Often times being in a hurry while stuck in traffic, I am reminded that maybe I'm being delayed from an accident that could be down the road. How many of the things that we suffer is really God watching over us so something worse doesn't happen?

5. <u>So that we might point others to God's amazingness</u>. 1 Peter 4:16 says, "yet if any man suffer as a Christian, let him not be ashamed; but let him glorify God on his behalf." Even though my life has been filled with many speed bumps I have had an equal amount of opportunities to share the good news of God's healing.

6. <u>So that we may identify with Jesus a little more</u>. Philippians 3:10 says, "That I might know him, and the power of his resurrection, and the fellowship of his sufferings, being made conformable unto his death." In the 50+ times I've been in the hospital, I have learned to look up and think of my Savior suffering on the cross of Calvary. My suffering helps me to identify more closely with Christ's suffering.

7. <u>So that your faith might grow a little stronger</u>. 1 Peter 5:10b says, "After that he have suffered a while, make you perfect, establish, strengthen, settle you." Every suffering that I've experienced helps me to put more faith in my cistern until now it runs over.

8. <u>So that others would see us and be compelled to follow us to Jesus</u>. 2 Timothy 2:10 says, "Therefore I endure all things for the elect's sakes that they may also obtain the salvation which is in Christ Jesus with eternal glory." I know that people watch us as we go through trials and sufferings. Our strength hopefully gives them strength.

9. <u>To make us an example of what a life trusted to God looks like</u>. Romans 8:28 says, "And we know that all things work together for good to them that love God to them who are the called according to his purpose." I have tried to live that life that prompts others to want what they see I have, but of course I have failed so many times.

10. <u>To move others to pray and depend on God for what only He can do</u>. 2 Corinthians 1:10-11 says, "Who delivered us from so great a death, and doth deliver; in whom we trust that he will yet deliver us; ye also helping together by prayer for us, that for the gift bestowed upon us by the means of many persons thanks may be given by many on our behalf." My life has been blessed with praying people. I would not have survived without them because it leads to what I call the circle of prayer. When people pray for you, they are really praying for God's presence in your life to heal and to help. Wherever God's presence is felt, there is a natural peace. If peace is there, that allows his power to work in your life. While His power is at work, He will reveal His purpose through it all. Once you understand His purpose for your struggles, that will lead you to the spirit of praise. The more you praise Him, the more of His presence will be felt as you complete the prayer circle.

11. <u>To train us to go to God first for health</u>. Psalm 30:6-7 says, "And in prosperity I said I shall never be moved. Lord, by the favor thou hast made my mountain to stand strong: thou didst hide thy face, and I was trouble." The old saying is true that when you're in a hole, stop digging. How many times have we tried to put something together only to get

stuck and have to go back and read the directions? Sometimes we have to go back and read God's directions to find our way. We often wonder how we got on the wrong road of life. God's Word is a perfect roadmap for life, but we failed to read it and heed it.

12. <u>To give us special experience of God's presence and an amazing story to tell others</u>. James 4:6-9 says, "But he giveth more Grace. Wherefore he saith, God resists the proud, but give us grace onto the humble. Submit yourselves therefore to God. Resist the devil, and he will flee from you. Draw nigh to God, and he will draw nigh to you. Cleanse your hands, you sinners; and purify your hearts, ye doubled mind. Be afflicted, and mourn, and weep: let your laughter be turned to morning and your joy to happiness." My life has been an amazing roller coaster ride with lots of scary times, but the high of experiencing God's presence afterwards has been worth every trial and every sickness. I can only hope that as I share my story, others will be drawn to the One who gives meaning to my life.

I have also learned 10 simple lessons from Robert Morgan's little red book called the Red Sea Rules. As the Israelites were standing on the shore of the Red Sea, I am sure they were wondering why God brought them to this point. They had the sea on one side and Pharaoh's army on the other and they were trapped in the middle. There have been many times I have felt this same way–like I was between a rock and a hard place. We need to remember that God always has a plan.

1. Realize that God means for you to be where you are. Tests your faith, teaches us wisdom, only God knows the reason.

2. Be more concerned for God's glory then for your own relief. God said, "I will be honored upon Pharaoh and upon all of his posts that the Egyptians may know that I am the Lord."

3. Acknowledge your enemy, but keep your eyes on the Lord.

4. Pray. We have a choice to either panic or pray. The situation by the Red Sea was crisis time prayer for the Egyptians and many times we are in that crisis mode.

5. Stay calm and confident, and give God time to work. Psalm 37:7-8 says, "Rest in the Lord and wait patiently for Him." We know that the phrase "fear not" is used 107 times in the Old Testament and 42 times in the New Testament.

6. When unsure, just take the next logical step by faith. Though they could not see Canaan or even the other side of the Red Sea, they realize they must take the first step in faith.

7. Envision God's enveloping presence. Exodus 13:21 says, "God gave a cloud by day and fire by night for God's people." Psalm 139:5-6 says, "Thou hast beset me behind and before, and laid thy hand upon me."

8. Trust God to deliver in his own unique way. Remember the Red Sea was a gateway for one and a graveyard for another.

9. View your crisis as a faith builder for the future. Faith: grow it and store for future trials so your cistern will be full and running over.

10. Don't forget to praise him once you are through the crisis.

39

Joys in My Life

Thinking back on my life has reminded me of many times it seemed like I was living under a dark cloud with storms around every corner. There were a lot of storms, but the sun did breakthrough on many occasions that gave me great joy.

A. Acting

I have always enjoyed acting. In high school, I was in five plays in four years. There was just something about playing a part where you could be someone else and say whatever the character's part called for. When the opportunity presented itself later in life to be part of the James Valley Christian school's annual dinner theater production, I welcomed the chance. In "the un-condemned", I played Simeon, the witty and cynical brother of Tamar (the woman taken in adultery.) In "No Name in the Street," I was a simple temple trader who got caught inside the temple when everything was disrupted by a madman, who later became known as Jesus the Messiah. The last production and most memorable for me was "Joseph". My character was Ymir, a camel trader who purchased Joseph and brought him to Egypt. Ymir watched as Joseph lived all of his experiences in Egypt. Ymir could not understand how Joseph could later forgive his brothers for what they did to him by selling him into slavery. Who knows in what ways God is preparing each of us to serve him in the future! Thanks to YouTube, everyone can watch his production of Joseph at <u>Joseph 2007a JVCS dinner theater presentation.</u>

Thank You for Your Gift

Ron Weidner (Ymir) Tom Brantner (Joseph)

What a joy and privilege to have been a part of the 2007 Stewardship Dinner Theater production, *Joseph*. Even though we did not see Ymir have a yielded heart to God, rest assured my heart was refreshed and rededicated through the message of *Joseph*. Oh the love and forgiveness shown to us through his life.

During the long days of practice, I was reminded again and again how God prepares each of us for some special time and place that we might be used for His purpose. May the words of Joseph ring in your mind as they have in mine:

"But who am I to question God?"

"Somewhere out ahead of me, there is something you want me to be. Beyond horizons I can see, somewhere I'll find my destiny."

"All my days, God has been preparing me in countless ways. He's been refining me, refining me all my days."

My prayer is that you can say with Joseph that God is refining you.

Ronald Weidner

Ron played the part of Ymir, trader and story teller. Ron is a James Valley Christian School grandparent.

B. Grandchildren

I must stop short of sounding like Garrison Keillor as he described the people of Lake Wobegon, Minnesota, as being the prettiest, the smartest, and all-around best people anywhere in the world, as I describe my grandchildren.

A. Andrew Blake (Sugarblock)

Not all grandparents are as blessed as we have been to have her grandchildren so close to us growing up. When our first born grandson came into the world, we were practically there in the delivery room. One of the true miracles on this earth is how a person can have such intense feelings of love for someone who has just arrived in the world. For some of us, this happens each and every time a new grandchild arrives. Shortly after Andrew Blake arrived in 1995, his parents moved to Huron, South Dakota (with some encouragement on our part). This gave Paulette a chance to babysit Andrew and of course she needed help from me! Having played basketball and coaching on several levels, my heart was set on helping him to become all he could be in the sport I loved. I owned a house with three apartments. My daughter and son-in-law lived on the main floor, my wife ran a daycare in the basement, and I ran my insurance office in the garage apartment. Every day Andrew would come to my office to shoot baskets into the plastic hoop I had set up in the living room. Since the ceiling was only 9 foot tall, Andrew frequently hit the ceiling scraping off the texture. I often did a terrible thing by offering him five dollars to make 25 free throws in a row. He was so persistent that my offer cost me a lot of money through time. I would also pretend to be announcing the final seconds in the state championship basketball game and Andrew had the ball. Counting down the seconds he would shoot before the buzzer went off and I would cry out, "Ulvestad shoots, and scores, and wins the state championship!!" He won third place in the nation shooting free throws at the National Elks Hoop Shoot in 2007 and won an all expense trip to Springfield, Massachusetts. Another thrill for me was to film and announce all his high school games as we streamed them on the internet. As a gift to him, I was able to give him a disc all four years of high school basketball. He was also fortunate to go to the State B basketball tournament in 2011, 2013 and 2014. As a senior, his team won the State Class B title. Although he did not make a last-second shot to win, he scored 15 points in the championship game in a 13 point win over the opponent. Of the 15 points, he made 9 of 11 free throws. All that practice shooting free throws at four years old paid off, and I was glad I spent many five dollar bills helping his dream come true. He was able to fulfill a dream that I always had. He has now completed his degree from SDSU. Andrew is married to his grade school sweetheart, Tara, and they have a beautiful son, Bentley Andrew.

A. Anna Marie (Snooks)

Anna Marie was born as I was flying to Fargo, North Dakota on a business trip. I could hardly wait to get home to see this beautiful little girl. As she grew up, I would tell her she had the most beautiful facial profile I had ever seen. Early on in her life, we could see she had real talent in swimming. For several years she competed and was fast moving up in her age group. With many ribbons and medals in her collection, we had high hopes of moving into state-level competition and being very successful. Often our dreams and our hopes of success in a particular area are shattered by our physical limitations. An injured shoulder that required surgery would put any dreams of future swimming success on hold. Pouring herself into other sports, she loved volleyball and was doing very well until an accident occurred that would affect her the rest of her life. Shagging balls during warm-ups in volleyball, she was hit in the side of the head with a spike, which caused a severe concussion. In spite of these setbacks in life, she is now a very gracious, beautiful, talented young lady who is a kind, loving person. I still refer to her as my Snooks with a beautiful profile and kind heart.

A. Ava Rose (Scooter)

Ava Rose was our 8 pound preemie who brought us to our knees in prayer because of her severe breathing problem at birth. My heart was broken the first time I saw her in that cloudy cube where she was laying, struggling for every breath she took. The doctor soon realized she needed more help than they were able to provide because her lungs were not quite developed. It was a wise decision to fly her to Sioux Falls, where they administered surfactant in her lungs. Her breathing was soon normal as her lungs were not stuck together, therefore allowing her to breathe. She required a month in the intensive care unit. Upon her release, we knew she needed to be isolated and not in a daycare. Since I was the only person who could put their work on hold, I was drafted as full-time care provider. The bonding that took place over that first year will forever be etched in my memory as a wonderful time. Feeding, changing, playing with Ava, as well as singing her to sleep as we rocked, will be for me a memory of a lifetime. What a joy it is to watch her grow into a teenager as she develops her many talents. Some of her many qualities are being loving, kind and caring for others. Yet to be fully realized are her love for basketball and volleyball. I also see great talent in running the 400 m in track... but she has not accepted that challenge yet. I thought it slightly strange that she watched cooking shows at such a young age, but soon realized she had an amazing talent for baking wonderful treats. I look forward to her junior high and high school years and I will be there to cheer for her as she strives to reach her full potential.

A. Gracie Joy (Spitfire)

Gracie Joy came into our family after my son and daughter-in-law waited years to have a child. We were given this gift from an unselfish mother who felt she could not raise her. Gracie Joy is an answer to prayer and we love her so much. One could tell by the nickname I gave her, "Spitfire," that she has brought a real spark to the family tree. Smart, determined and talented are just a few of her many qualities. By her actions in the first few years of grade school it looks like she will excel in many sports, including golf. Paulette and I are very hopeful that we will be around to watch her compete in many activities as she goes through school. If determination and fight are any indications, she will definitely be among the winners.

C. Fishing

One of the other great joys in my life has been to have two brothers and several other very close friends that have enjoyed fishing with me. From Lake Erie, Lake Michigan, Minnesota Lakes, Lake Winnipeg Canada, Alaska, local lakes and all along the Missouri River, we have fished. The 20+ years at our cabin in Akaska, South Dakota would certainly be the highlight of all fishing. The trip to Alaska served as a trip of a lifetime. Even though we missed many Sundays in church through the years, I have always kidded people by saying "it is better to be fishing and thinking about God, than being in church and thinking about fishing." Fishing and catching always brought two joys to me. Not only do I love to fish, but I also love to give the fish away to people who love to eat them. Being on the water on a calm sunny day, viewing God's great creation, always brings me back to the things that are really important in life. When you are at peace with God, at peace with your fellow man, and you have a loving family waiting for you back home, one could lay back, soak up the sun and live in that moment forever. That is until your rod bends and you feel the tug of a lifetime at the end of your line, and you're hoping this could be the big one!

Fishing in Alaska

Ron and his boat on the Missouri

D. The God pocket

For the last few years I have carried around a small pouch in my wallet that contains what I call God's money. Of course I supply the pouch with whatever has been laid on my heart. Recently I have been carrying a $20, $50 and a $100 bill. The principle is to pray how God might introduce me to someone in need as I go about my days. The need may be financial, but could also include just sharing or helping someone in need. Armed with this mentality, a person is able to go through his day wondering when God will provide someone in need. There is a certain anticipatory joy that comes with this challenge. Once you have helped meet a need, it often opens up the opportunity to explain how Christ has led you to act accordingly.

The article in our local paper did a great job of explaining this concept. Since the Mennonite foundation first brought it to my attention, I have shared with many others. The winning story about my snow removal concept led the foundation to award the $5,000 to me for distribution. Over the last five years, I have many stories of how God uses these gifts to bring joy and hope to others.

CONTRIBUTED

Ron Weidner, center, presents checks for $500 each to Brian Held from James Valley Christian School, and Kristi Brantner, director of James River Royal Family Kids Camp. Below, Weidner, right, presents a check for $1,000 to Jon Duba, director of Byron Bible Camp. The money is from the Mennonite Foundation, which sponsored a contest Weidner won sharing his experiences with the God Pocket program.

Sharing through God Pocket

BY CRYSTAL PUGSLEY
OF THE PLAINSMAN

Reaching out to help another person who looked like they needed a hand has always been second-nature to Ron Weidner of Huron. That's one reason he was so intrigued by a "God Pocket" challenge issued last fall by Jon Wiebe, president of the Mennonite Foundation.

Written by Bruce Wilkinson, "God Pocket" encourages people to carry money in a special spot in their purse or wallet and to give this money to someone they see who needs help or just the encouragement to know that God cares for them.

"He said we should do this, and be put out a challenge," Weidner said. "Put money in your billfold and depend on God to lead you to the right person."

As part of the challenge for members to adopt the God Pocket principal, the Mennonite Foundation also asked people to share their stories of God Pocket giving. Weidner won the top prize, $5,000 to be given to his favorite charities.

Whether it is reaching out to someone in line at the grocery store or encouraging a waitress struggling to begin a family, there were many instances when giving someone an unexpected $20 bill and the message that God cares for them lit a spark of hope in their eyes.

Weidner decided to submit his story to the contest promoted by the Mennonite Foundation about passing on the God Pocket idea to his neighbors.

"In the winter I clear about six driveways in the neighborhood," he said. "They wanted to know what they could do for me, and I gave them a God Pocket brochure and asked them to help brighten someone else's day."

The Mennonite Foundation handles the $5,000 award, issuing checks as Weidner directs.

So far, he has given $1,000 to Byron Bible Camp, and $500 to James Valley Christian School for playground equipment and $500 to the Royal Family Kids for camp scholarships.

The additional funds will be held until next year to help support the above three entities.

"I had helped people with heating and electric bills before, but it wasn't part of my regular giving program, just a spur of the moment thing," Weidner said.

"With God Pocket, you're searching for what we call the nudge, a sense that this is the person we are to help," he said. "That is interesting and exciting."

Weidner said he keeps $20 bills in a certain spot in his wallet that he can give.

"There might be days where I don't see anybody," he said. "I leave that up to the Lord; if I feel that nudge I go up and follow through."

Weidner said he gave his God Pocket money to a store clerk one day who was having a difficult day, and another woman, who was shopping with her children and picking up food and putting it back on the shelf. "I said, 'This is God's money, and He wants you to be encouraged,'" he remembers.

"It's exciting just to get out and be looking," Weidner said. "I'm looking for something, and I don't know who it is or where it is — but you get that nudge and you want to help."

Weidner said he has been sharing his experiences with fellow members at Bethesda Church. Weidner and his wife, Paulette, have two children and four grandchildren.

"I started telling my Sunday school class about it, and several of them are doing it," he said. "This has changed my attitude. It's been a learning experience.

"The joy in people's faces — just giving them hope is something," Weidner added. "It's fun — the joy of giving. Other people have caught that spark, and hopefully, it will spread."

40

About the Author

I was born and raised on a simple country family farm in Beadle County near Yale, South Dakota. A person could say I was born in a time of great tragedy. With the death of my dad, mother carried me during this time of great agony in her life. Having described her experience of going from death pains to birth pains I am reminded of how the power of the human spirit is able to endure so much.

Thrust into a new family structure I struggled with loneliness of where I really belonged. I was very fortunate in that my stepdad treated me very good. There were never any harsh words or spankings or lectures which I'm sure I deserved on many occasions. I have no memory of ever hearing harsh words of rebuke from him. There was also silence when it came to any kind of feelings of love or encouragement.

My years of grade school were spent at Johnson school about 2 1/2 miles from our farm. I have already described my four years at Yale high school in some detail. It has always been a cool joke to tell people that I am a Yale graduate but not finishing the story by saying it was only high school. The next four years at Huron college were very trying years but I managed to get a degree one day and get married the very next day. It was during the next eight years of teaching, counseling and coaching that we added to our family a son, Tracy Paul and shortly thereafter a daughter Lea Marie. My wife had told our family doctor, also our dearest friend that she wanted a dark-haired girl. When the Dr. delivered our baby to the room he just shook his head and said "I don't know how you were able to get just what you ordered but here she is."

The next few years after leaving Iowa were spent in a rural farmhouse with me working at Huron College. My termination at the college fell at the same time my stepdad passed away. With great optimism I stepped into a new role as full-time farmers. The next 20 years might be called my "wow years" because I would have never believed that so many things could go wrong in that time. As time progressed I became more involved in our church by teaching, being on the deacon board and also involved in the Board of Education. On several occasions I was asked to preach in area churches as well. Our pace of life came to a halt with cancer being discovered in my wife's ear. Shifting from a farm operation to a full-time insurance business required a new focus. The business of life and the extreme economical pressure I was under during the farm years did untold damage to our family. With lack of finances and always clawing our way out of various holes our kids were often the brunt end of our frustration and lack of understanding.

Since then both of our children have taken wonderful God-fearing spouses and given us four outstanding grandchildren and one great-grandson. We now work towards rebuilding any damage that might have occurred in those early years. Not knowing the full extent of my family's past spiritual history, I now strive to ensure that all of my family going forward has an experience with Jesus Christ as I have had in my life.

Moving to the sunset years of life I fully realize that we need to give up a few things that tie us to this earth. I'm in the process of getting rid of our last rental property. The Lord has blessed us over the past 25 years with various properties we have owned. After enjoying our cabin by the Missouri River for the past 20+ years we realize that part of our life must also end. My brothers and I have enjoyed many fishing trips together as well is great food and fellowship there.

For the past 10 years we have lived in Huron, South Dakota where we are members of Bethesda church. I am semiretired but occasionally I do get calls to help settle claims for the insurance company I have worked with for the past 20 years. My passion has been to share the gospel with all who have needs. The "God Pocket" concept has been something I have been involved in for about five years. When occasions arise I encourage people to attend the program at church called celebrate recovery. This program is for anyone who has hurts, habits and hang-ups that they are struggling with.

It is my hope to finish my race strong while serving my Lord and Savior Jesus Christ. My challenge for each reader is for you to finish strong as well. Use the light within you (whatever the size wattage of the bulb within you i.e. the love you have for lost souls) to shine in the dark corners of other's lives to give them hope. May it be said of you and me when we are gone that he brought light to others wherever we walked.

Ron and Paulette and family through the years

About the Author | 193

CPSIA information can be obtained
at www.ICGtesting.com
Printed in the USA
FSHW021046131020